LOVE OF LOONS

Kate Crowley and Mike Link
Photography by Peter Roberts

KEY PORTER BOOKS

To Howard and Alta, Ann and John
With love

Published by Key Porter Books, Ltd.
70 The Esplanade, Toronto, Ontario M5E 1R2 CANADA

First published in the United States by Voyageur Press Inc.

ISBN 1-55013-063-3

Printed in Singapore by Singapore National Printers Ltd
through Four Colour Imports, Ltd., Louisville KY

5   4   3   2

CONTENTS

FOREWORD

*L*ove *A Loon* reads the bumper sticker on the car I am following in stop-and-go traffic in downtown Minneapolis. I smile to myself cynically. Perfect. Here this person is adding to the fossil fuel consumption problem, acid rain with his exhaust, urban sprawl, and my headache. And he says, "Love A Loon." How absurd. If he really cared about loons, he'd walk or take a bus.

Two blocks and five minutes later, I realize that it's no more absurd for him to be driving than for me. My truck doesn't sport a sticker proclaiming my love for anything, but I care about loons as much as he. Probably more. Why am I adding to the problem?

It's a long drive to Chequamegon Bay from the Twin Cities. As I get out of the suburbs and the towns that are too close together to tell where one ends and the next begins, my headache subsides and I think about the man in the car and his bumper sticker. He probably really does care about loons, but like many other people he is trapped in a lifestyle that doesn't allow him to live near a loon lake and that forces him to contribute to acid rain and other problems confronting loons. His actions may not reflect it, but I'll bet he really does love loons.

As a wildlife biologist, I'm not supposed to love loons. Emotions lead to subjectivity, which taints what are supposed to be objective and unbiased attitudes and decisions. Love a loon and lose the respect of the scientific community, intolerant of such weakness.

A problem arises. How am I supposed to control or ignore the emotions that theoretically make me a poorer biologist, when it is the strength of these emotions that guided me into a career in wildlife conservation? I ponder this and drive on.

I'm on the edge of "loon country" in Wisconsin. From here on, I can keep my eyes open for loons on the lakes the road takes me close to.

My tired eyes and back tell me to pull over to a rest spot near Hayward. Eyes closed, I lean back against the front bumper and listen to the early afternoon winds in the pines. Then I hear the faint yet unmistakable "whoosh-whoosh" of a loon in flight. Yes, it's a loon. The sound and cadence of wingbeats are right. The trees prevent any sight of the bird until it's right over me, and then it's gone behind the trees on the other side of the road. I clench my fist, shake it, and utter a muffled "all right." My spine tingles.

I catch sight of Lake Superior just west of Ashland. "Shining big sea water." I've resolved that it's okay to be a biologist and love loons too. In fact, I'm convincing myself that to be a good biologist one *has* to love loons—and coyotes and oak trees and black flies and bats. If I lose my emotions, my convictions that the world is a better place with loons (and all other creatures), I will have lost the ingredient that fuels my fires.

As a biologist, I know a lot about loons, their habits, and what makes them tick, but this isn't what motivates me. Rather, like almost everyone who has heard loons' mournful wails in the still of the night or has watched their ritualistic antics on a northern lake, I am spellbound by their magic.

I guess I'm destined to love loons.

PAUL STRONG
Biologist, Sigurd Olson Environmental Institute, and coordinator of Wisconsin Project Loon Watch

ACKNOWLEDGEMENTS

No book is the product of one or two people. As authors, we have to draw on the collective wisdom of our culture. We read other books, we search the literature for researchers' discoveries, and we talk to experts who have insight to add to what we read. These chunks of knowledge are assimilated, then shaped by our experiences as teachers, naturalists, and outdoor enthusiasts. Ultimately, we have the responsibility of deciding what to pull together to share with you, the reader.

The publisher, the editor, the designer, and the various photographers all influence the book's shape and final look, creating a package of information meant to give you the easiest, most enjoyable dose of knowledge that we can.

In this acknowledgment, we of course want to thank a number of people for their help. But we want to accomplish more than that: We want to let you see the tracings of our tale and to introduce you to some of the special people whom we have encountered.

Clifton and Rita Herreid were kind enough to invite us into their cabin and to share with us the experience of caring for "Looney." Jimmy Pichner and Mike Don Carlos shared insights into the efforts of raising a loon at the Minnesota Zoo. Carrol Henderson, of the Minnesota Nongame Division of the Department of Natural Resources, let us review his files, shared correspondence, and gave us good leads. Pam Perry, of the Brainerd DNR office, gave us more leads to follow; Mike Loss, also of Brainerd DNR, gave us an interview that explained his reports and added the rich personal knowledge he has gained as a game farm operator.

We called Dick Shabert, Roy Tasche, and Rick Julian because they built nest platforms and each was willing to give us a full description of his observations. Bill Bauer, director of the Northwoods Wildlife Center in Minocqua, shared the Center's stories; and Jack Mooty, of the Grand Rapids DNR office, related the information that he gathered while flying loon counts.

Peter Roberts contributed more than photos—he shared many of his observations from the blind. Gary Dulin, of the University of Minnesota, wrote of personal experiences that relate to his research. Kim Eckert, of the Minnesota Ornithologists' Union, brought us up to date on the name change of the Arctic and Pacific loons.

Paul Strong, of the Sigurd Olson Environmental Institute and Wisconsin Project Loon Watch, added great richness to our work. He gave us personal anecdotes from his study in Maine, he offered us the Institute correspondence, and he volunteered to read this manuscript for accuracy. We greatly appreciate Paul's support and work.

As writers, Kate adds her experience as a naturalist at the Minnesota Zoo, where she worked for nine years, and Mike contributes the knowledge he has gained as director, instructor, trip leader, and naturalist at Northwoods Audubon Center for fifteen years. We are both grateful for the knowledge that we have accumulated at these places.

It is our job to synthesize, to breathe life into the facts, to give you new information, and to entertain you, too. We have made arbitrary decisions about what we think is important. We have had fun and we have learned a lot. We talked to people in Minnesota, Maine, Massachusetts, Vermont, New Hampshire, Michigan, Wisconsin, and Illinois and enjoyed these new acquaintances. Now we are eager to make *your* acquaintance. We hope you will help make the environment a place where people and loons can live together. We will know you by your actions. Join the clubs and organizations that we mention. Observe and enjoy. Make a difference.

CALL IT ARSEFOOT

The word *loon* has many connotations, and those who wouldn't consider reading this book might think of some of the other meanings first. Why do we call the bird *loon*?

I can understand *whippoorwill* and *phoebe* — they name themselves by their calls, but the loon does not call out "loon, loon." Kirtland's warbler, Townsend's warbler, Franklin's gull were all named in honor of some scientist or friend of the scientist who first described the bird, but there is no Fred's loon in the ornithological lists. Black-and-white warbler, black vulture, and red-tailed hawk describe colors; curve-billed thrasher and fork-tailed flycatcher describe both physical characteristics and behavior.

The word *loon* and its etymological relatives have been used for many purposes. If someone calls you a loon or says, "Don't be loony," you can decide which of the following meanings is appropriate.

From the Old Norse language, *loon* is derived from *luenn*, which meant "beaten, benumbed, weary, or exhausted." It also appears in the phrases "false loon" and "to play the loon," a fifteenth-century Scottish use, which meant "to be a rogue or a scamp." *Loonery* was the mischievous acts of a rascal.

Loon could also mean "strumpet or concubine." The poet Scott used it this way in his line "the gayest, grittiest loun." This meaning, and various spellings, appears from time to time in literature from 1590 to 1800.

Sometimes, *loon* referred to a person of low rank: "lord and loon." From this meaning we evolved the loon as a boor. Others used the same word to describe a boy, lad, or youth.

The word *loon* bounced around the English tongue, seemingly in need of a definition. In one geographic text, an area of clay domes is described as having "been formed ages ago into butts or loons, varying from 15–50 feet."

In Scotland, there was a mark (coin) worth a hangman's fee; it was called a loon-slatt. In America, our western storyteller Brett Harte gave the word *loony* a new meaning. In his classic work *Heiress of Red Dog*, he wrote, "You're that looney sort of chap that lives over yonder, ain't ye?"

Somehow, this word took a separate path to our diving bird. Originally, the loons were known as the great northern divers. They also had a rather descriptive name that indicated the placement of their legs, far back on the body: arsefoot. At various times, the bird was also called a black-billed loon, didapper, dipper, dobchicker, and doucker. Another descriptive name was great speckled-diver.

It was almost a perfect match — a word without definition and a bird without an official name. In 1634, W. Wood wrote in *New England Prospectus*, "The loone is an ill shaped thing like a cormorant." In 1672, in *New England Rarities*, the name was used again to describe "a waterfowl akin in shape to the wobble."

In the tangle of words and their roots, *loon* as the name for the bird may have taken a completely different path of evolution from the other questionable uses.

Seamen in northern waters called the guillemot and the diver *looms*, or as it was sometimes recorded, *lumme, lumb,* or *lumne*. The *Oxford English Dictionary* says that *loon* comes from a Shetland dialect. This word was used in a nautical sense for objects that loom on the horizon.

Others believe that *loon* comes from the Icelandic *lomr*, which translates to *lame*, because the loons are so awkward on land with their "arsefoots." This same ancestry applies to the word *lummox*, which describes a big, awkward person.

Now the bird influences our perceptions of the word, and in the twentieth century we can be called "crazy as a loon" because of its wild laughter. *Lunatic*, which comes from *luna*, or moon, is "loonatic" in some people's language. Since full-moon nights are good nights for loon singing, and folklore says that the insane are worse on nights of the full moon, the

(P. Roberts)

term "loony bin" combines our thoughts on both derivations.

In Mexican waters, where some of the loon species spend their winters, the loon is called *somorgujo*, a word that comes from the Spanish verb for "to dip or dunk (dive)." *Somorgujo* is used for mergansers as well. If our other meaning for *loon* is translated south of the border, it becomes *bobo*, "a fool."

Our loon names don't stop there. We also have the Latin names to consider. Their order is Gaviiformes, family Gaviidae, and genus *Gavia*, which means "gull" in Latin. A man named Forster, for whom the Forster's tern is named, chose the genus. He left no explanation. Previously, the genus had been *Colymbus*, from the German word *kolymbis*, which meant "diving bird." Linnaeus, the originator of the binomial language, gave it this older genus. For awhile, *Colymbus* covered both grebes and loons; then it was lost altogether.

P. L. Hatch, state ornithologist for Minnesota, in 1892 recorded the family and genus as *Urinator*. This was a short-lived genus name between *Colymbus* and *Gavia*. It is from the Latin *urinator*, "a diver," and had been used by the French naturalist Cuvier as early as 1800.

The yellow-billed loon, also known as the white-billed loon, is *Gavia adamsii*. The great American biologist Asa Gray named it in honor of Edward Adams. Like its common name, the red-throated loon's Latin name is descriptive of its physical appearance, *Gavia stellata*, which means "starry gull." In the winter plumage, the bird's back has a spotty appearance, reminiscent of stars.

The Inuit have many names for these birds, but most refer to the pointed bill and translate to "having tusk": *tuutlick*. The Cree called the loon *Mookwa*, the spirit of the North. At Fort Chimo in 1880, Lucien Turner reported that it was called *kashagat*, which comes from the cry of the loon.

Our common loon is *Gavia immer*. *Immer* is from the Latin *immergere*, "to dip, plunge into, dive," the root for such English words as *immerge* and *immerse*. This species name is one of the few parts that make sense. But "common"—never! Maybe I'll mount a new campaign for *Colymbus immer*—the speckled arsefoot.

THE LOON'S PAST

THE LOON IN PREHISTORY

Ten Pleistocene fossils, representing four of our present-day loon species, were reported by Gerald Fitzgerald in the *Canadian Journal of Earth Sciences*. The fossils were found in the Old Crow Basin in the northern Yukon Territory, an area that is in the range of the common, Pacific, and red-throated loons today. One of the Pacific loon fossils was found in beds more than 54,000 years old, a period that geologists call the Sangamon interglacial age. Two of the red-throated and the yellow-billed loons had minimum ages of 10,700 years. All of these loons were identical to their present-day counterparts. These were "our" loons, the same spectacular colors, the same vocal variations.

It's hard to imagine our loons without us, but there they were, thousands of years ago, near the area that our human ancestors used as a gateway to the North American continent. The loon watchers were wearing furs and progressing to their own place in the continent's ecology.

The loon actually has been here for a much longer time than the human species has even existed. The loon occupies a space in the front of the bird book because it represents the most primitive of today's birds. It is an early adventure in evolution, and its line dates back to a time when existence was totally different than today. Life in the Mesozoic was primarily aquatic. The land masses that we know as continents did not have either the size or the location that we know. All of our modern birds, Ornithurae, evolved in that aquatic environment. A bird field guide shows the order of evolutionary development.

To trace the path of loon evolution, we must go back one hundred fifty million years to find a primitive animal that we call the archaeopteryx. Whether it was reptile or bird is still debated. It flew, ran, and glided just over the forest floor. It had teeth, and feathers that were modifications of its reptilian ancestors' scales. It took to the air, where the insects had held dominion. Life would never be the same again.

Scientists debate over why birds evolved at all, why the scales turned to feathers and the birds left land. Initially, they speculate, the feather form of scale was an improvement in insulation for birds and protected them against a changing climate. Then the early feathered animals found that they could sweep the ground with their "wings" and gather food. Through accident of locomotion, flight was discovered, and the effect on the ecology was dramatic. For example, the smaller insects had a better chance of survival against the new hunters in the sky, so small species flourished. With evolution and modification of existing life-forms, the newly developing lineage of the bird diversified, too, to fill the various niches that were available. They split into species and variations as food and climate changed. They competed with one another for food and space.

Fifty million years after archaeopteryx, two new fossils fill in blanks on the earth record—*Ichthyornis*, a strong flyer and fish eater much like our modern tern, and *Hesperornis*, a large fish eater that lost its ability to fly as it adapted to the water environment. While most people do not see these as direct ancestors of the loon, they were important experiments in filling the loon's niche.

As with the modern genus of loons, there were four species of *Hesperornis* swimming in the Cretaceous seas. Their fossils were found in Kansas and Montana. *Hesperornis* looked like a loon, but it was six to seven feet long and had teeth in its bill. Flight was impossible for a bird built like this.

Some people debate over the accurate placement of *Hesperornis* in the animal families, and many contend that it was in fact a mosasaur, a type of dinosaur. (There are also those who contend that all birds are really relict dinosaurs.) Joel Cracraft, of the University of Illinois, published a paper in 1982 that attempted to prove that *Hesperornis*, *Baptornis*, and a number of extinct genera were in fact a single lineage, and he claims that the loon is most closely related to the penguin. Other scientists put the loon as an offshoot of the Charadriiformes, a group that includes the shore-birds, gulls, and auks.

Whatever the answers to questions of development and relatives, we know that the very style of life that today's loons have was an effective means of survival throughout the evolution of most of our continent's life-forms.

In Kansas and Colorado, in the Dakota sandstone of the lower Cretaceous, we can find tracks that are our earliest North American records of the true birds. A bird known as *Enaliornis* is the oldest known *Hesperornis*-like bird. Its fossil, found in England, indicates that it was a marine bird similar to the loon, with high specific gravity and feet set toward the tail. Its feathers were probably furry, like the loon chick's.

The modern loon family has the longest record of the current families of birds. Their fossil record goes back to the Paleocene, about seventy million years ago, the period immediately following *Hesperornis*'s demise.

In the Paleocene, the Appalachians had a few peaks surrounded by a level peneplain, and the Rocky Mountains were just on the uplift. The Yellowstone area had two major lava flows, which incorporated the deposits of marine life between them (an indication that the sea dominated this area even with the volcanic activity). There were also lava flows in the Columbian plateau. The Canadian shield, the region that is now considered to be the common loon's home territory, did not have the thousands of lakes that we know today. It was a land of rivers and streams, old mountains, eroding rocks, and dry landscapes.

All our present forms of plant life were in existence at this time, but not in the places that we would now expect them. Cypress was found throughout the loon's present territory. The loon lived in the sea, where life was varied and abundant. It fished its way through millions of years while the continent slowly grew, shapes shifted, and glaciers etched and sculpted the lake basins that dot the North.

Now the loon is a twentieth-century species, an animal of the Holocene, just as we are. We have lost the little ten- to twelve-inch *Colymboides minutes* that was found as a fossil in the Miocene beds of France, *Colymboides anglicus* of England and the Oligocene, and *Gavia concinna*, *G. howardae*, *G. palaeodytes* and *G. portisi* of the Pliocene, but the loon genus has withstood all the changes of seventy million years. With a little understanding, it may make another seventy.

THE LOON IN HISTORY

"As they offered conspicuous and attractive targets for rifle practice and were wholly unprotected, either by law or by popular sentiment, it was customary to shoot at them whenever opportunity offered. Often the progress of the steamer up the lake was indicated and proclaimed by the frequent popping of guns fired from her decks at Loons and other water-fowl." ("The Loon on Lake Umbagog" by William Brewster, *Bird-Lore* September-October 1924.)

The current love we have for the loon is a fad. Fads are variations from the normal patterns of society, and that is why they stand out. The loon's popularity stands out because of our cold indifference in past generations.

Arthur Cleveland Bent, in his classic work *Life Histories of North American Diving Birds* (1919), wrote, "The breeding range of this species is becoming more and more restricted as the country becomes cleared and settled, the loons are being gradually killed off or driven away. A pair of loons nested in Quittacus Pond, Lakeville, Massachusetts, about 14 miles from my home, in 1872, but the eggs were taken and both birds were shot; none have nested in this section of the state since. The same story is true of many another New England lake where the insatiable desire to kill has forever extirpated an exceedingly interesting bird."

Our land-use history has been one of extreme contradictions. While we produced two of the world's greatest ornithologists, Alexander Wilson and John James Audubon, we were also eliminating the Carolina parakeet and the passenger pigeon.

Thomas Roberts, Minnesota's most famous ornithologist, wrote in 1932, "The Loon, or Great Northern Diver, is a summer resident throughout the state. It was formerly much more abundant than at present and every clear water lake was the home of a pair of noisy loons. Its steady decrease has been due, in great part to the fact that this large bird has ever been the favorite target of the man with the gun or the rifle."

In 1766, Jonathan Carver, a Mississippi River explorer, wrote, "It was ill-favoured flesh, but excellent sport."

Through our years of development and growth, the loon moved from sport to enemy to symbol of the wilds. In the first half of this century, the inland fisherman knew that the loon ate fish, and fish meant money. Loons were shot, along with mergansers, grebes, and cormorants, because they took too many fish. Today most know better. The fish that the loon takes are rough and small fish, fish that have no commercial value.

The hope for the future is that the loon fad is also a trend, a change brought about by greater knowledge, and that our concern will last beyond the commercial aspects of the fad. We have dedicated people, land owners, naturalist–resort owners, and naturalist–tourists, who are learning about the loon, its ecological role and its uniqueness. These personal commitments will extend far into the future, with other generations building on today's knowledge. Perhaps the trend is best observed through the writings of our best-known naturalist-writers, for their works reflect not only our state of knowledge but our ethics.

THE NATURALISTS

"If ever so slightly wounded, the Loon prefers diving to flying off, and all your endeavors to kill it are almost sure to prove unavailing . . . a method of shooting these birds, which I have often practiced, and which was several times successfully employed . . ."

The author of these words goes on to describe how to "toll" a loon, that is, to conceal oneself, wave a brightly colored cap or handkerchief, and imitate the bird's calls. When the loon is close enough to be easily shot, the gun finds its mark.

It is well known that the loon has in the past been hunted for "sport." Should we be surprised to discover that many of the early naturalists—men whose thoughts and accomplishments we very much admire today—were out there shooting loons? The opening quotation is taken from the writing of John J. Audubon, who is famous for his bird paintings. He and Alexander Wilson were responsible for the beginnings of North American ornithology. The above quote occurred in the early 1800s, a time when all game was thought to be in endless supply and this new country was a "sportsman's" playground. Throughout the nineteeth and well into the twentieth century, this attitude prevailed.

John Burroughs was a New York nature writer who influenced Theodore Roosevelt and created the East Coast's environmental conscience at the turn of the century. He described the loon as having "something almost supernatural in his alertness and amazing quickness, cheating the shot and the bullet of the sportsman out of their aim." The loon was considered a great challenge because of its wariness and speed of escape. It was not generally hunted for food— Audubon said the meat was "tough, rank and dark colored," although he did see it served and "relished by many lovers of good-living, especially in Boston, where it was not unfrequently served almost raw at the table of the house where I boarded."

It was the challenge of the hunt that prompted the young John Muir to shoot a loon. The bird was trapped in a small pond that was most frozen over. Muir retrieved the wounded bird and carried it home. He placed it on the kitchen floor and watched as it sat, perfectly still, full of dignity and wariness. In the minutes that followed, the family tomcat, which had also been observing the loon with great interest, inched its way closer. The bird almost imperceptibly cocked its head, so that when the cat was a foot and a half away, the head and pickax-like beak shot forward and struck the cat square in the center of the forehead. The cat somehow survived the attack, and both he and John Muir developed a great deal of respect for even a disabled loon.

John Muir went on to gain fame for his thousand-mile walk from Indianapolis through the Smokies and down into Florida, his rambles in the Sierra Nevada, and his expeditions to Alaska. He was the West Coast equivalent of John Burroughs, but much more active. He founded the Sierra Club and Yosemite National Park. He was the torch bearer of Emerson and Thoreau and used his pen to create a national park system. However, for all his ramblings, it was a loon on Fountain Lake, Wisconsin, that turned his heart. He never shot anything again. Through the loon, he learned a deep love and respect for all of nature.

Another record of a revered naturalist hunting the loon comes from the late 1800s. John Burroughs wrote that "the loon laughs the shotgun to scorn," but his hunting party had with them a breech-loading rifle, "which weapon is perhaps an appreciable moment of time quicker than the ordinary muzzle-loader, and this poor loon could not or did not dodge."

At least he seemed to feel some sadness for the fate of the loon; he wrote, "The bird I killed was a magnificent specimen, and I looked him over with great interest." He goes on to describe the bird in great detail: "His glossy checkered coat, his banded neck, his snow-white breast, his powerful lance-shaped beak, his red eyes, his black, thin, slender, marvelously delicate feet and legs, issuing from his muscular thighs and looking as if they had never touched the ground, his strong wings fell forward, while his legs were quite at the apex, and the neat elegant model of the entire bird, speed, and quickness and strength stamped upon every feature—all delighted and lingered in the eye."

We need to remind ourselves that during the era in which these men lived, the possibility of human-caused animal extinction was not even imagined. Loons were just another bird to be taken, put on display, and admired in home or museum. It wasn't until 1934 and the advent of the *Peterson Field Guide* that most people's attitude began to change and observation of living birds was considered more desirable than admiration of stuffed ones.

Not all the early naturalists hunted the loon, however. Some were content just to attempt to get close to a live loon. In October 1852, Henry David Thoreau was paddling on Walden Pond when a loon presented itself about 50 feet in front of him. Thoreau paddled in the direction of the bird, but the loon dove and surfaced even closer. A quick dive put it 275 yards away; and no matter how hard Thoreau tried to calculate where the loon would emerge, he never again got closer than a hundred feet. He spent an hour just sitting in his boat and watching the loon dive and surface, announcing its presence each time with "his unearthly laugh."

All of these naturalists were great observers of the loon's behavior. John Burroughs noted that when a loon in flight lands, "it plows into the water like a bombshell." He also tells the story of a loon that lived in an enclosure with a grebe in Bronx Park. On a winter day their pool froze over except for a small hole in one end. The grebe dove and did not immediately resurface. The loon soon followed, swimming to the end where the grebe was. There the loon swam hard for the surface and struck the ice with its bill, piercing the frozen crust. It swam down again, turned, and swam upward with enough force to shatter the ice and create another opening. The grebe followed. People that witnessed the event were certain the loon had gone to the rescue of the grebe, which seemed to be trapped below. Burroughs cautions against becoming too anthropomorphic, and quotes a man by the name of Hamerton: "The moment we think of [animals] as human, we are lost."

Audubon, through observation of "at least 20 pairs" of loons, debunked a belief that during breeding season the birds "dart down suddenly from the air, and alight securely" on the nest. He writes that by closely observing a loon, the student of nature "cannot fail to derive much pleasure from watching it as it pursues its avocations."

Audubon suggests, "View it as it buoyantly swims over the heaving billows of the Atlantic, or as it glides along deeply immersed, when apprehensive of danger, on the placid lake, on the grassy islet on which its nest is placed; calculate, if you can, the speed of its flight, as it shoots across the sky; mark the many plunges it performs in quest of its finny food, or in eluding its enemies; list to the loud and plaintive notes which it issues, either to announce its safety to its mate, or to invite some traveller of its race to alight, and find repose and food; follow the anxious and careful mother-bird, as she leads about her precious charge; and you will not count your labour lost, for you will have watched the ways of one of the wondrous creations of unlimited Power and unerring Wisdom." From that description, you realize that the man spent more time observing loons than shooting them.

Moving into the twentieth century, we discover that some of our more recent naturalists have employed the techniques of old to observe loons more closely. Edwin Way Teale tells how one afternoon he and his wife sat beside a pond "tolling" for a loon. "Nellie thrust her hand outside the car window, waved a white handkerchief in the sun, then drew her arm inside again. The loon turned toward us." For more than ten minutes they "played this ancient game of the gunners" until the bird was about fifty feet from shore. That evening they watched the same loon, this time with its mate, going through a courtship dance. "The paired birds rushed across the water in an almost upright position, sitting on their tails, then, close together dipped and bobbed their heads in a nuptial display. It was a moving spectacle, these loons, the oldest in line of ancestry of all living birds, engaging in a display that extends back through millions of years, accompanied by the same wild cries that men of the Stone Age heard in the dusk of evenings infinitely remote."

When John McPhee came upon a loon in the wilderness, he watched closely as the bird gave a laughlike call. "The bird's lower jaw opens and claps shut five times in each laugh. If, from where you watch, he is swimming in silhouette, you can count the movements of the jaw. . . . a long cry in the still of the night . . . is made with the neck stretched forward, and it is a sound that seems to have come up a tube from an unimaginably deep source — hardly from a floating bird." McPhee became so engrossed in the loon and its laugh that he responded in kind. "The loon is laughing again, so I laugh back. He laughs. I laugh. He laughs. I laugh. He will keep it up until I am hoarse. He likes conversation. He talks this way with other loons. I am endeavoring to tell him that he is a hopeless degenerate killer of trout. He laughs."

Of all our generation of naturalists, the one who has had the most association with the loon is Sigurd Olson — a man who spent a major portion of his life in prime loon territory. Olson lived in Wisconsin during his youth and in Minnesota as an adult. He was a college instructor and dean, an ornithologist, and a canoeing guide. He was the spokesman for the Boundary Waters Canoe Area, and for him the loon was synonymous with the wilderness lake country. Over the years he had many encounters with loons, made many observations of their behavior, both the commonly known and the startling. Once, while crossing a portage with a canoe on his back, he was confronted with a black and white "apparition . . . standing bolt upright" on the trail. The loon was just as surprised as Olson and turned to rush madly away, "half flying, swimming and running on its ridiculously tiny legs" back to the water.

Kekekabic, Burntside, Knife, Lac La Croix, and Lower Basswood Falls are but a few of the canoe country places where he watched the birds and listened to the wild harmony that a group of loons can create when moved by the spirit of camaraderie.

At Listening Point, where Olson had a small cabin, the early morning and evening hours could be spent watching a pair of loons in the little bay. From ice-out in the spring, when the loons first arrived, till late fall, when they gathered in large numbers farther out in the lake, Olson would watch and listen. He compared their calls to the howling of huskies and wolves, the yodels of people calling in the Alps, and just pure "wild rollicking laughter."

Anyone who has ever heard a loon call on a clear northern night, or watched one dive and magically reappear half a lake away, will feel the same thrill and wonder that all of the great naturalists felt. We can identify with their words and agree wholeheartedly when Sigurd Olson says, "Without the music of their calling and the sight of them on the open water, the lakes of the north would never be the same."

LOON LEGENDS

That the loon would become the source of myths and legends is not surprising. A bird whose distant melancholy cry can evoke such strong emotions and identification with human feelings, a bird that can disappear from the surface of a lake just a few feet away from us and moments later pop up hundreds of yards away, has the makings of magic. The loon is a shy bird, which prevents close observation of its habits and behavior and so allows much room for speculation and imagination.

(P. Roberts)

John Burroughs reports that "Scotch fishermen will tell you that the loon carries its egg under its wing till it hatches. One would say they are in a position to know; their occupations bring them often into the haunts of the loon; yet the notion is entirely erroneous."

Archaeological evidence indicates that loon folklore has survived from the days of the Old Stone Age. In Ipiutak, Alaska, graves from early Inuit cultures have included skulls of loons with carved ivory eyes set into the sockets, staring with the same intense look as those set into the human skulls. A possible explanation for the loon's inclusion in the graves with the people is that the loon was to act as guide, to escort the spirit to the netherworld. Even into this century, the old people of the Faroe Islands believed that the call of the red-throated loon flying overhead meant that it was following a soul to heaven. The connection to death and the afterlife also is found in the Norwegian belief that loon calls foretell that someone will be drowned, attributing the strange sounds to ghosts and water spirits, and in the Ojibwa belief that the call was an omen of death.

Based on the legends that are told about the loon and the variations that have developed, it is believed that stories spread from Asia to America. In a circumpolar path, the stories are told from eastern Finland and Latvia, across Asia, and into North America. Among the Siberian peoples, wooden images of loons were erected on coffins, and loon images decorated the clothing worn by shamans.

Shamanism and loons were closely intertwined throughout the northern cultures. The loon aided the shaman on journeys to the spirit world, which was sometimes believed to be underwater. The shaman has always been believed to be able to control the weather. This belief, along with the loon's close association with shamanism, has gradually been diluted but not lost. Now fishermen look at the loon as the local weather forecaster — a common belief around the globe.

In Shetland, the red-throated loon was called the rain-goose because of the belief that it is especially vocal before a rain or bad weather. The Norwegians believed the same. The Thompson Indians of North America claimed not only that the loon could predict the rain but that, like the shamans of old, it could cause rain to fall. John James Audubon came upon this belief while on a voyage from Charleston to the Florida Keys in May 1832. He says, "There is an absurd notion, entertained by persons unacquainted with the nature of this bird, that its plaintive cries are a sure indication of violent storms. Sailors in particular, are ever apt to consider these call-notes as portentuous. . . . I several times saw and heard loons travelling eastward; but not withstanding all the dire forebodings of the crew, who believed that a hurricane was at hand, our passage was exceedingly pleasant."

When a creature is thought to have close ties to the supernatural, it is held in high esteem and treated with respect. Among some Inuit groups, the severed head of a loon was worn as a talisman, giving the wearer manly qualities. Newborn babies were wiped with skins of loons so that they would be assured of health and long life. The Yakuts and Buriats of Siberia would not kill loons nor disturb loon nests for fear of disaster befalling the people. The Siberian Tungus people considered loons sacred and would not even mention their names. Norwegians considered it disrespectful to kill loons.

Unfortunately, the same cannot be said about the Europeans who settled the United States, or their descendants. The folklore of Maine includes what is meant to be a humorous story, which has variations across the country, relating to the hunting and cooking of waterfowl. Occasionally a hunter shoots a loon — usually for the feathers or skin. The recipe for cooking a loon is as follows. "Flay a loon, clean it, soak it and place it in a large pot with salt and pepper to taste. Add potatoes, turnips, onions, and other vegetables. Add one large granite stone about the weight of the bird. Place the pot on the stove and allow it to simmer for five days, adding water when necessary. At the end of this time, remove the container from the fire and allow it to cool. Remove the loon, throw it away, and eat the rock."

The Ojibwa have a loon clan, or totem. A totem is a means of identification within a tribe, based on blood and kinship and classified by a symbolic animal, fish, bird, or reptile; it could be compared to a European coat of arms. The totem descends in the male line, and intermarriages never occur between persons of the same symbol or family, even from different and distinct tribes.

Mahng was the Ojibwa word for loon, but the totem family name was Ah-ah-wauk, derived from imitating its call. They claimed to be a chief, or royal, family, basing their assertion on the fact that nature had placed around the neck of the loon a collar that resembled the royal necklace worn by a chief, which is the badge of his honor.

The legends about the loon can be broken down into three categories: the story of creation, the story of how the loon got its voice, and the story of how the loon got its colors (feather patterns).

For the Ojibwa, there are different versions of the creation story. In one, the loon attempts to fetch mud from the bottom of the flooded earth, drowns in the attempt, but is resuscitated. In another, beaver, otter, and muskrat fail to get the clay, but the loon dives and brings some up on its feet. For the Samoyed of Siberia, the story of the flood includes the loon. Seven men escaped in a boat; and seven years later, a loon brought up some mud, which the men threw into the water, so causing earth to appear.

The Arikara creation legend is called How Corn Came To Earth. Mother Corn was leading the chosen people to the west, as the god Nesaru had directed her to do. They came upon many obstacles in their path, and various animals came to the rescue. One obstacle was a large lake, too deep and wide for them to cross. The people considered turning back, but "a waterbird with a black head and checkered back" appeared and told Mother Corn, "I am the Loon. I will make a pathway through this water. Let the people stop crying. I shall help them." Then, like a winged Moses, the loon swam so quickly through the water that the water parted and the people walked across to the other side. After crossing, some of the people chose to stay and became loons.

Among the Algonquian, the legend of how the loon got its voice is as follows. Kuloskap (known as Gluskap to the Micmac), the Master, was hunting on a lakeshore when he saw a loon flying low over the water. Two times the bird circled the lake, swooping low over Kuloskap.

"What are you looking for?" Kuloskap demanded.

"You," replied the loon. "Are we friends?"

"Yes," answered Kuloskap.

Then Kuloskap taught Loon how to call his own special cry. "You shall be my messenger. When I need you, I shall call you thus. When you want me, call thus." Since that day, loons are faithful to Kuloskap forever.

The Ahts say the loon and crow were once two fishermen who quarreled when they were out to sea in their canoes. The one who was unsuccessful in fishing knocked the other on the head, cut out his tongue, and stole his catch. When this poor man reached shore, he could only cry like a loon. The Great Spirit transformed him into one, and the aggressor became a crow. Ever since, when the loon was heard calling with its sad wail, people would know it was the unfortunate fisherman trying to tell his sad story.

The legend of how the loon got its "necklace" and feather pattern is one that is known with slight variations by Inuit from East Greenland, Labrador, Central Canada, and Baffin Island, as well as Indians of the Northwest and some Athapascans of the interior. Traces of the story are even recorded among the Plains Indians. The Tsimshian version tells of an old man who was blind and could not support his wife and son because he could no longer hunt. He went to the water's edge to call to the loon, whom he knew to be a wise and magical bird. The old man sang a sad song, "My heart is breaking with grief."

The loon heard and replied, also with a sad song. He swam to the old man and asked how he could help. The old man told of his plight and said he would give his prize possesion, a shell necklace, to see once again. The loon told the man to hold onto the bird's wings and bury his eyes in its feathers. The two dove into the water and surfaced just as the man felt his lungs would burst. He could see the shape of trees after that dive. They dove again, and this time after surfacing, the

man had regained his full vision. He was so overjoyed that he pulled the necklace from around his neck and tossed it to the loon. The bird's feathers had been completely black, but as the necklace fell around the loon's neck, a white pattern was created. Some loose shells fell on the loon's back. Wherever shells touched, white marks appeared.

In the story there was also an old hag who created some problems for the family. In the spring the old man, his sight now restored, wished to escape from the hag, who had turned herself into an annoying owl. He and his family decided to leave, but as they did, they heard the loon calling from far away. Now it was no longer a sad sound. The old man told his family, "The Loon is laughing. How proud he is of my necklace."

In the Bering Strait Inuit version of this legend, it is a young boy who has been made blind by his evil, jealous mother, who is a witch doctor. He seeks out a loon and dives into the water three times, the third time with the loon. His sight is restored and his joy is great. In this version the loon receives no necklace, just assurances from the boy that the spirit of the loon shall always be the favorite spirit of his children and grandchildren.

A third Inuit legend on how the loon got its colors involves the loon and a raven. Both are white, and they have agreed to tattoo one another. They begin by putting stones in a circle and building a fire, letting it burn down to charcoal. The charcoal is pounded to a powder and put in a stone box. Loon patiently waits while Raven decorates him, making markings on his wings with a piece of bone dipped in the charcoal. Raven finishes, and Loon begins to tattoo him. Raven complains about the designs, and is restless, shifting from foot to foot, twisting his neck and fluttering his wings. Loon finally loses his patience, picks up the box of charcoal, dumps it over Raven, and runs away. Raven is very angry, picks up a fire stone and throws it at Loon, hitting him in the legs and injuring him, so that he can hardly walk. Ever since, the raven has been all black and the loon looks as though he is about to fall whenever he tries to walk.

The myths no longer seem part of our society, until we analyze how we perceive the animal. Aren't our images reflections of the mysticism that we still associate with the bird? We still hear stories of loons flying with their young on their backs, we still tell ghost stories at the fire with the sound effects of loon laughter in the background. Fishermen still think the loon took the giant fish and that's why they didn't catch it. Loon figures, loon-costumed people, join Woodsy Owl and Smokey the Bear as modern images. Times have changed, but we still seek ways to express our relationship to the earth. For the generation of the '80s, the loon is a magical, mystical symbol.

The common loon. (P. Roberts)

THE LOON TODAY

The loon has taken on a significance that goes beyond its beauty as a bird, the biology of the species, and the struggle for survival. The loon is ingrained in today's society, a measure of our concern for the land, our relationship with water, and our pleasures in the wilderness. Its echo is important to the cabin owner as well as to the canoeist who paddles the remote landscape of the Northwest.

In the past, loons did not have the status most ducks did. They were not good eating; they weren't part of the hunting literature or art. They were shot in tremendous numbers just because they were a challenging target, but that can hardly be called sport. For years the loon was just there, an expected resident on wilderness lakes.

The loon has had some special recognition, from Tattler, who was the eyes and the ears of the creator in the religion of the eastern Canadian Indians, to Longfellow's *Song of Hiawatha*, where the great honor of being named Loon Heart (*mahn-go-taysee*) is bestowed on Hiawatha at a feast. *Mahng* in this text is used as the word for both "brave" and "loon" in the Ojibwa language.

We have tried to look at the loon with some perspective. Although we revere the bird today, we are still killing it as we did in the early part of the century. Today our means of killing isn't as obvious as rifles on excursion boats; now we use chemical warfare, acid rain, mercury, and lead. While we kill the loon with these tasteless, unseen poisons, we also kill ourselves.

A generation ago, the eagle was brought back from the edge of destruction. We recognized its beauty and its place in the wild. We decided then that we wanted to maintain our national symbol for future generations and we protected it from the gun and from the poison of the time, DDT. Now the eagle is back, and in some places is common. But we get reports that the eagle is harassing the loon, bothering the chicks and distressing the adults. Some now question whether we should protect the eagle so much if it is going to bother the loon.

We hope that people will see the loon in the broader sweep of natural history—that it is much more important to preserve the loon's role in ecology than just a stuffed animal. If we want to set a goal, let's make it a goal that allows for eagles harassing loons, with plenty of both to assure that they will all survive into the distant future.

Perhaps an Ojibwa song sung just before going into battle is the best song for all of us. Like all Ojibwa songs, it is simple, with the emphasis on how the words fit into the melody, and states something that is obvious, but desired, since it represents strong medicine.

Kiwitagicig	Flying all around the sky
Gabines imoyan	The loons are singing

SPECIES

Today we recognize five species of loon: common, Arctic, yellow-billed, red-throated, and Pacific. The Pacific is a recent addition to our U.S. checklist. It was separated from the Arctic loon by the American Ornithologists' Union in 1984. Except for a few Alaskan migrants, all the sightings of the Arctic loon in the U.S. have probably been Pacific loons rather than Arctic, but the bird-watcher had better keep new records, rather than change the past notations. For our book, we will leave the Arctic and Pacific data as one group and refer to them as Pacific loons. Research has not caught up sufficiently with the split to allow us to really differentiate behaviors in the two birds. It is enough to know that they are different.

The winter bird-watcher should look for a definite thin chin strap at the back of the loon's chin, a field mark that is not present in all Pacific loons, and a white patch at the flank near waterline, which is present on Arctic, but not Pacific, loons. This patch is like that found on the common loon, so more observation of the winter bird is necessary to tell if it is a Pacific loon. If the decision is between the common and the

The red-throated loon. (© Steve Krasenann/Nat'l. Audubon Soc. Coll., PR)

Pacific, the best indicator is to watch them dive. Common loons simply dive forward, but the Pacific loon stretches its neck up and erect to its full length before going underwater. In breeding plumage, all the birds are easier to distinguish. The Pacific loon has a purple iridescence on its throat and the Arctic has green.

The loon is one of three distinct freshwater diving birds; the grebes and the mergansers are the others. The grebe's almost nonexistent tail sets it apart from the loon, which possesses a short but definite tail, and the grebe has lobed toes rather than the fully webbed foot of the loon. The mergansers are ducks with bills that are flattened and serrated on the edges for both grasping and straining. Mergansers and loons share many northern lakes by dividing the territory. There doesn't appear to be a clear habitat distinction.

TAKING COUNT

"The common loon is so conspicuous that it often appears to be more abundant than it really is." (*Life Histories of North American Diving Birds* by Arthur Bent, 1919.) It is large, dramatically colored, and vocally obvious. If we don't stop to consider that the loons are limited to the deep lakes, that they share only the largest bodies of water with other pairs, and that they reproduce very few young, we might overestimate their actual population and status.

In 1974, the Audubon Society of New Hampshire and the Squam Lakes Association determined that a study of loons was needed. The population was low and there had been a decrease of 53% in lake utilization. In 1976 and 1977, New Hampshire initiated a study to census their loon population.

The census confirmed their concerns. Scott Sutcliff and the Loon Preservation Committee took canoes and small motorboats onto every lake that they thought could handle a loon and counted every nest that they could find. With perseverance, they were able to cover most, if not all, the loons in the state.

In 1977, New Hampshire loons maintained eighty-seven territories on forty-five lakes. Sixty birds produced thirty-eight fledged chicks; there were forty-nine nest failures. Most chicks that were lost died in the first two weeks after hatching.

Records indicated that there had been sixty-eight lakes that supported loons within the prior fifty-year period. In 1977, only thirty-two of these were nested on. Some of the other lakes supported nonbreeding adults. The decrease was due to loss of habitat, increased human activity, and increased nest depredation by raccoons, dogs, cats, and other animals whose population increased with human development. (Raccoons, which have had a dramatic population increase due to human development, destroyed forty-nine nests in 1977.)

The New Hampshire experience generated a nationwide awareness. Inventories and observations took on new significance. Judy McIntyre, a researcher

The yellow-billed loon. (© *David Hill/Nat'l. Audubon Soc. Coll., PR*)

The Pacific loon has long been known as the Arctic loon in this country. The differences in appearance between the two are very subtle. In breeding plumage, both have a dark gray face, blending into a lighter gray head. The black throat patch has a purple iridescence in the Pacific loon (above) and a green iridescence in the Arctic (below). On both loons, the back is mostly black, with black and white patches near the wings and upper back. The top photo of the Pacific loon was taken in Alaska by Kenneth Fink (© K. Fink/Nat'l. Audubon Soc. Coll., PR). The lower photo of the Arctic loon (black-throated diver in Europe) was taken in Scotland by David Hosking.

who pioneered loon studies in Minnesota before moving to Utica College of Syracuse University, had in 1971 begun Project Loon Watch, which enlisted people throughout Minnesota in a record-keeping procedure. She encouraged people to watch loons with greater interest and to record their observations.

Local people who lived on lakes, and cabin owners, volunteered to keep records of loons on their lakes. They observed the first arrivals, last migrants, and reproduction. Three hundred twenty-four lakes were included in the first report.

The reports gave good data on changes in individual loon populations on the studied lakes but were limited by how frequently the lakes were observed. There was an inconsistency between lakes where the observers were residents and lakes where observers were only occasional visitors. And the observations lacked scientific controls. There was nothing to indicate that loons used one lake for feeding and another for nesting, nor did the study account for the nonnesting birds. It was a start, but not enough.

In Wisconsin, the Sigurd Olson Environmental Institute of Northland College took the initiative for loon research. They instituted a Project Loon Watch similar to Judy McIntyre's and began to assemble data on the loons. Little was known about the distribution or status of loons in Wisconsin at the time the project began in 1978. Their first goal was just to record any sighting they could and to enlist "cooperators" in a network of observations. (One year later a UW–Stevens Point graduate student completed a master's degree project documenting the approximate size and distribution of the Wisconsin loon population.)

The network grew with a speed that surprised and overwhelmed the Institute. They were not set up to handle the response, and the result was the development of a data collection system that grew faster than the biologists could design it. They wanted to take advantage of people's willingness to work, so they sent out forms similar to those already in use. The reports were biased by the volunteers' natural choices: There was no observation of lakes without loons, because counters would not choose them, nor of the truly remote lakes, because people were not living on them.

In 1983, the Institute studied a random selection of lakes over thirty acres in size from the northern twenty-eight counties, considered the primary loon range in Wisconsin. From the reports of 720 volunteers on 874 lakes, the population was estimated at 2500 to 3000 birds for the state.

It was a start, but it lacked the controls that are necessary for a completely accurate study. The observations were made over two months. There was no accounting for movement of birds and no grouping by lake size, which would allow for a more accurate projection figure. Because the survey covered two months, first and second nests created a variation in observations. The count did not address the most important statistic, reproduction. With long-lived birds

and low adult mortality, population drops can be delayed by adult survival. Older birds may stop reproducing, but still show up in the annual counts, which means that periods of poor reproduction may not affect the overall population until there is a sudden drop sometime in the future.

The Institute took a second count in 1985, and the estimated population figure was 2200 to 2500. As with the first count, its accuracy was plus or minus hundreds, and it can't be taken as anything other than a comparative figure for counts by the same method.

Paul Strong, the current Institute biologist, says that Wisconsin Project Loon Watch is not trying to "track the size of Wisconsin's loon population. Rather, the project is trying to help lake residents keep track of and protect the loons that inhabit their lake. The current monitoring program focuses on collection of specific information about the loons and human activity on individual lakes. The rationale is that Wisconsin's current loon population is large and well-distributed. Barring a large-scale disaster, the loon population will not change drastically over a short period of time.

"In Wisconsin, the highest priority is to identify lakes with loons and the location of nests and chick rearing areas. By collecting these data as well as information on land ownership, the status of shoreline development, recreation levels, and causes for nest failure or chick mortality, WPLW can advise the appropriate public agencies and private individuals about future lake development, such as the placement of boat access ramps. Slowly the program is changing to one where the cooperators are the eyes and ears of the Institute and even more importantly, the grass-roots educators."

In Minnesota they are taking this lesson one step further. The Nongame Division of the state Department of Natural Resources is involved in monitoring the loons' activities. They replicated Judy McIntyre's survey in 1986, the fifteenth anniversary of the original study. That is only a small part of the effort that they are putting into loon habitat analysis, air counts, and other loon studies. The department is encouraging the building of nest platforms and banding of loons, and is sponsoring a Loons On Loan educational program.

The Sigurd Olson Environmental Institute has put in a companion program, one that is different from their own Wisconsin program and that is intended to supplement the Minnesota DNR effort. The Institute has formed the Minnesota Loon Preservation Project to establish Loon Rangers, similar to those in the New Hampshire program.

Their hope is that the Loon Rangers will help in communicating with and educating the people who live in and use the area where the loons nest, to reduce harassment. The project will eventually do population estimates, too, but that is not the most important effort. The real impact will be on the home lakes of the Loon Rangers. They will be activists; and to be effec-

tive, they will also be educated. Agencies can study and manage, but they can't totally protect the loon. Only people can do that, and only public concern can move local and state government units.

In Vermont, 1983 was a pivotal year in the loon program. Their inventory of breeding loons had been conducted by the Vermont Institute of Natural Science for seven consecutive years. The physical survey involved 620 person-hours. Lakes of appropriate size and lakes with a past history of loon use were chosen. Then on one day a count was made. Volunteers in canoes and boats and on foot checked fifty-four lakes, observing loons and talking with fishermen and residents.

The total for the day was thirty-nine: twenty-nine adults, one immature bird, and nine chicks. There was an overall decline from the 1982 projected population of seventy-two to 1983's projection of forty-six birds. The decline had been steady since 1979, when ninety birds made up the Vermont population. The good news was that the breeding success was at its highest level since the survey began, 29.4 percent. But the question was, is the breeding success sufficient to offset the overall population decline? Since it takes loons three years to reach breeding age, the answer would not be known for a number of years. Vermont declared the loon a state endangered species.

The loon has a range that extends through the states that border Canada. In 1985, Washington had two or three pair of breeding loons. Idaho had one known pair and a dozen nonbreeders, Wyoming had four pair on its northwestern border, and Montana had seventy to one hundred nesting in and near the Glacier National Park area, an area much closer to the red-throated loon's territory than the common loon's. North Dakota had a small pocket of loons in the Turtle Mountains area along the border. Massachusetts had five or six pairs on the reservoirs for the city of Boston, and New York had three to four hundred in the acid-rain-devasted area of the Adirondacks. Michigan declared its population threatened.

The remaining major populations were in Minnesota, Wisconsin, and Maine. For those three states, visiting every lake to count the loons, like they did in Vermont and New Hampshire, was out of the question. They needed a different strategy.

To count the loons, Minnesota and Maine are turning to the airplane. With lakes deep in the wilderness, volunteer ground counts are not completely effective. Wisconsin, with little wilderness and many lakes, has a different situation.

Maine did a three-year study, 1983 to 1985. The state was divided in half, with most of the southern lakes counted by ground observers and planes covering the northern half. That left them with the problem of correlating the results from the two methods.

The ground observers conducted their count from 7 to 7:30 A.M. on July 20. The flights covered seven routes at an altitude of two to three hundred feet. The planes made a single pass and had to contend with wind, sun glare, fatigue, and plane speed. There was no way they could separate mature and immature birds under the circumstances.

In 1984, four lakes were counted simultaneously by both methods. After five repetitions, the figures showed that the aerial counts were only 50 to 73 percent effective. In 1985, counts of fifty-five lakes were duplicated, and the count consistency was 47 percent.

The Maine count did confirm the fact that loons prefer the larger lakes. The statewide estimate was 3950 loons, but the errors in counting are too great for this to be any more than a comparative figure for future counts by the same technique.

Minnesota's project, with Jack Mooty, is similar to Maine's, but concentrating more on the technique to increase accuracy. Mooty discovered that the plane had to stay on the lake for a longer period of time, because often the loon would dive in response to the plane's approach. There was no way for the single flyover to catch nest sitters, divers, or birds in the shoreline vegetation. Mooty and his pilot collaborate on the count, observing loon reactions, the angle of sun and wind, the time of day for making the count, and the configuration of the lake basin.

The flight counts still need refinement, just as the land methods do, but they represent our concern for this beautiful species and our awareness of the loon's position in the northern states. As for the loon, each day that the Minnesota crew takes off, a loon on the lake where the plane is based displays to the big float-plane. It is unwilling to share its territory with the big metal bird, science or not.

(P. Roberts)

If a loon perceives danger to the young, it gives the tremolo call—the call described as the loon's laugh. Notice the throat pouch beginning to expand on this adult loon as it begins to call. (D. Cox)

SONG AND DANCE

For as long as people have wandered and lived near northern lakes, they have turned their heads to look for the source of the soprano uvulations coming off the waters. These sounds evoke strong feelings of empathy and emotional identification. The Cree heard in them the anguish of a dead warrior denied entry to heaven, and the Ojibwa interpreted the cry as an omen of death.

The loon has a basic collection of four calls that can be given individually or combined to signify the response to conflicting emotions. Very often the call is given in combination with a physical display—what might appear to be a type of dance. Because we find such emotional and spiritual feelings in the loon's repertoire of calls and displays, it may come as a shock to learn that three of the most commonly heard calls are vocalizations of excitation, stress, and distress and therefore reflect negative conditions, rather than celebration.

In the 1970s William Barklow undertook a serious study of the loon's vocal communication. His research resulted in a doctoral thesis and a popular recording, *Voices of the Loon*. Much of what we understand today about the loon's moody music is based on his study.

The four calls are described as (1) wail, (2) yodel, (3) tremolo, and (4) hoot. Most people are familiar with the first three calls because they are the most dramatic and easily heard. The hoot is a softer monosyllabic note, with a questioning, tentative sound to it. It is given by an individual bird as it approaches a flock, or when surfacing with food for a chick. It appears to be used to locate or keep in contact with nearby birds. On a misty morning, it is a sound one might hear and have trouble identifying, for it has none of the dynamic qualities that we normally associate with the loon. The hoot is the call that we hear least frequently.

Most people who have written about the loon, including the earliest naturalists, have described its wild "laughter." While he was on Wrangell Island, John Muir wrote, "A loon flew past as we lingered, scream-ing and making the solitary place more solitary by his intensely lonely wild laugh." This is the tremolo, a call with the characteristics of a hysterical soprano. Barklow says it can best be described as "a distress call . . . generally given in situations that are alarming to the bird."

A boat approaching a nest area will almost certainly cause the birds to tremolo, and the pitch and frequency will increase as the perceived danger increases. If a loon is suddenly disturbed while on the nest by an approach from land, it will quickly leave the nest and run on the surface of the water away from the nest while giving the tremolo call. When a loon begins to run across the water to escape another loon or human intrusion, the tremolo can be heard gradually fading into the distance, but the air continues to vibrate to that staccato syncopation.

A mated pair of loons will perform a tremolo duet if they should be near one another when confronted by a boat or any other threat to their nest or young. When birds duet, it is very difficult to distinguish one bird's call from the other's, for the calls are just marginally spaced apart and very close in pitch—too close for the human ear to distinguish easily—This asynchronous call may add to the intruder's auditory confusion and subsequent distraction.

It is during this type of encounter, when a boat or intruder penetrates a pair's territory and offspring are nearby, that the most dramatic display occurs. Some call it "penguin dancing." In this "dance," the loon rushes toward the intruder and rises, with head drawn back and bill almost touching breast, while its feet beat the water and create a spray around its body. The loon then falls forward, raising more water. It may momentarily dive, then rise again and beat the water with its wings, all the while tremoloing loudly.

One or both parents may display in an effort to create a scene of frenzy that will scare away or distract the threat to their young. To unenlightened human eyes it is a magnificent demonstration. However, as each

The most dramatic display of the loon is known as "penguin dancing." This behavior indicates extreme anxiety and is performed when the nest or chicks are believed to be in danger. Photographer Dan Cox was within telephoto camera range when this loon began to react to an approaching boat. We show these photos to help people recognize when they are in the wrong place and causing great stress to the birds. (D. Cox)

year passes, fewer and fewer people who visit northern lakes can claim ignorance of the true meaning of the birds' display. It should be an immediate signal that they have ventured into an area where people are totally unwelcome and should quickly withdraw.

When one loon of a mated pair returns to the nest, it may tremolo briefly. In this case, the call may be a means of strengthening the pair bond or may give reassurance to one another after a disturbance.

Loons in flight, when passing over another loon's territory, generally tremolo, the only call given by a flying loon. It has a distorted quality that contributes to its urgent sound.

The yodel is the most complex of the calls. It is believed to be given only by males, most frequently when establishing or defending territories, and it is considered to be an aggressive call. Anywhere from one to nine repeat phrases may be given—the greater the number, the greater the bird's agitation. It generally lasts four to six seconds, similar in length to some of the more complex songs of the warblers, but not as cheerful and upbeat. The yodel is the call heard most frequently around dusk, the time of peak flight activity. It appears to be a contagious sound. One loon may begin to yodel after an earlier aggressive interaction, and loons in surrounding lakes will pick up the call until all the woods and the night sky reverberate with the excited wild sound.

William Barklow, through his study and use of sonograms (paper graphs that visually record a bird's call, similar to the machines used to record heartbeats), believed that individual male loons could be identified by their yodel. He observed female loons joining a mate after hearing his yodel. By recording these calls and playing them back at a slower speed, or observing the sonogram, he could distinguish individual idiosyncrasies. These appear to remain the same from year to year.

Based on Barklow's research, further study has taken the loon's call into the computer age. Today another researcher, Ed Miller, at Governor State University in Illinois, is taking yodel sonograms from loons in the Sylvania Recreational Area of the Upper Peninsula of Michigan and putting them into a computer to more accurately catalog and identify individual birds. The purpose of this process is to see whether the same loons are returning each year to the same lake. Vocal recording is much easier on people and loons for identification and study purposes than is capture and banding of birds.

A display is associated with the yodel; Lynda Rummel and Charles Goetzinger, who studied loons in Ontario, call it the "crouch-and-yodel" display. The loon hunches low in the water, extends its neck and head so that it rests on the water, tips the bill up slightly, and yodels. After vocalizing, the loon returns to the normal alert posture of floating, with head held high. Rummel and Goetzinger observed this behavior most frequently when there were territorial confrontations between pairs. Loons have also been observed

yodeling when floatplanes begin to take off or fly low over a lake.

The last call is the wail, a melancholy, drawn-out sound that is most often compared to a wolf's howl. In 1857, at Walden, Thoreau wrote, "This of the loon—I do not mean its laugh, but its looning,—is a long-drawn call, as it were, sometimes singularly human to my ear." The wail is structurally like the tremolo, but lacking the modulation. It can carry farther on the wind than the other calls. Barklow speculates that the wail may have developed before the tremolo and that over time, as a more specialized communication signal was needed, the tremolo gradually evolved. Loon researcher Judy McIntyre has observed that the first vocalization of a loon chick is the wail.

Unlike the tremolo and yodel, the wail may be given in a variety of situations. In most cases, it is given when interaction is desired but somehow prevented, such as when a bird is searching for a mate or chick, or when a parent bird is separated from its chick by a boat. A female will wail when her mate is having an aggressive encounter with an intruder and while he is giving the yodel.

In early spring and summer, the wail may be the lead-in to a rousing night chorus. This chorus may be initiated by one pair of loons, then taken up by other pairs on nearby territories until sound echoes and fills the night sky. The mixture of yodels and tremolos, varying in intensity and tempo, seems to be tied to the general enthusiasm and excitement of the nesting season. The chorus may fade to a gradual conclusion or stop as abruptly as when a needle is lifted from a record.

Loons are also known to combine calls to cover more complex situations and emotions. It is not understood why, but these combined calls always begin with the tremolo. When it is combined with either the yodel or the wail, there is conflict within the bird—indecision, such as the fight/flight reaction that can be found in many other species. The combined call differs from a chorus in that it is a statement by the bird and not a chorus combining individual calls.

Loons perform one other display, which has the appearance of a stately minuet. It is called the "circle dance," or the "bill-dipping ceremony." It involves two or more loons and is frequently seen in large flocks as a greeting behavior or an appeasement activity. This ritual also can be seen in early summer as part of the loon courtship. In this dance, the birds swim toward one another, frequently putting their faces in the water in a peering motion. As they draw nearer to one another, they begin quick dives, sometimes together and at other times alternately. They submerge for only a few seconds and then surface very near to one another. They swim slowly in a circular pattern, occasionally "breast-puffing and bill-tucking," as Rummel and Goetzinger described it. If a bird dives and surfaces too far away, the dance breaks up and the rest of the birds paddle away. For a courting couple, the dance is the lead-in to copulation.

During courtship, a pair of loons perform the circle dance, or bill-dipping ceremony. They swim near one another in a circular pattern and occasionally dip their bills in the water, as if peering. (P. Roberts)

Most of us are familiar with the common loon, but the Pacific and the red-throated loon also engage in their own song and dance. Both have calls that are distinct from the common loon's, but difficult to describe. Perhaps the best way to relate to their various dances is to let your imagination flow with the descriptive names that researchers have given to the various movements. The Pacific loon displays are called the tuck, threat, and upright positions, the splashdive, and the threat dance. More inspirational are the red-throated loon movements: looking into the water, snake ceremony, and plesiosaurus race ceremony.

The loons are showy birds. Their feathers lack flamboyant colors, but make up for that with a striking, intricate, geometric black and white pattern. They dance on the water when consumed with desperation

and they fill the northern regions with echoes of antiquity. They inspire us humans to think deeply about ourselves and this planet. Their song has inspired the Paul Taylor professional dance company to choreograph a dance called "Sunset."

But they are not feathered vaudevillians put here for our entertainment. William Barklow has recorded the wail of a loon as it searches through a thunderstorm for its chick or mate—the sound of rain mixing with that plaintive call. He has recorded coyotes howling near a lake where loons spend the summer and superimposed the howl of the canid with the wail of the water bird. It's powerful enough to send shivers up the spine and tears down the cheeks, a sound we should hear in person, with water lapping at our feet and the pines pressing at our backs. As Bent so aptly said, "And what would the wilderness be without it?"

One sound parent loons use to communicate with their young is the hoot; another is the "mew." Chicks make a soft chirping sound. (P. Roberts)

THE LOON FAMILY

What is the purpose in all the wailing, yodeling, and displaying? Why migrate thousands of miles? Why fight off all other waterfowl? What is the reason for this annual ritual? It is all for the purpose of building a nest, laying eggs, raising young, perpetuating the species. That is why a pair of red-throated loons showed absolute devotion to a spiral-shaped sea shell in 1984.

The proud parents were faithfully attending the seashell in their nest when two researchers in Wolf Bay, nine miles west of Cape Whittle, Quebec, first observed this unusual incubation. They watched the birds for five days and there was no reduction in their faithfulness during that period.

There was no sign of broken eggshell to indicate that the seashell was a replacement for a failed brood. A gull might have dropped the shell to crack it, and it fell into the nest, but the shell was too old to have been good for gull food in the current year. It was a worn shell that had acquired a polish from the birds' efforts to hatch it.

The researchers watched for five days and then had to wrestle with their consciences. In the end they decided to liberate the two potential parents and threw the shell out.

NESTS

All the loons have very specific nesting-site requirements, which vary from species to species. The common loon prefers island nests. For a research paper on loons in Alberta, Kees Vermeer found that out of twenty-six located nests, twenty-five were on islands and one was on the mainland. Of the twenty-five island sites, twenty-two were wooded and three were treeless. In the classic study of loons in the Superior National Forest, Sigurd T. Olson found that fifty out of fifty-four nests were on islands, with four on the mainland.

Common loons situate their nests next to the water if possible. Deep water right up to the nest is prefera-

ble, to keep from exposing the nest when the adult approaches or leaves. If necessary, they will locate the nest as much as four feet away from the water.

The island nests may be built on muskeg, but the majority of those studied in Alberta were on sand, clay, or rock. The island protects the loon from their main mammalian predators, skunks and raccoons, as well as many of the secondary predators such as mink and fox.

Common loons will nest on lakes that do not have islands. In a British Columbian study, nests were placed into three categories: muskrat houses, shore sites, and floating sites. Canoe country has beaver instead of muskrats, and the beaver lodge may work in the same way that the muskrat house does. Lodges provide the loon with a modification on the island theme. In addition, the muskrat lodge usually is surrounded by emergent vegetation that works as a screen, allowing the loon to sit on the nest and face the rat channel with confidence.

In Maine, another nest-site variation was found: backwater areas such as the inlet and outlet streams of lakes, where flow was steady but very slow, almost to the point of stagnation. Loons nesting in these areas had greater reproductive success than loons nesting on islands or mainland sites. On lakes without islands, these areas were preferred nesting areas.

The common loon also has a strong affinity for its old nest. Paul Strong researched the use of habitat by common loons in Maine and found that birds tended to gravitate toward sites where previous nests had been placed. On ten lakes there were sixty-five territories that were reoccupied by loon pairs annually. The pairs did not necessarily nest every year, but they did occupy the same areas of the lakes. When they did nest, they typically used an old nest bowl or a site close by. Some territories had only one nest site, used year after year. Others had as many as four sites, used over many years.

In one extreme case, the loons built a nest near an

old submerged nest bowl. They laid their eggs in this new nest and incubated in an irregular manner that seemed to indicate less than the normal strong nest attraction that the common loon is known for. As the spring waters subsided, the old nest became visible; the pair moved to it, laid an egg, and began to incubate. The researchers watched this activity and moved one of the eggs from the first nest to the second. Both eggs were hatched. A sidelight to this is the fact that the second egg had been neglected for almost ten days and was still viable. This may mean that the birds' eggs are adjusted to the possible stress of fluke northern storms and that the loss of heat is less critical before the embryo forms.

Denny Olson, of the Minnesota Loon Preservation Project, is concerned by the reduction of water level in reservoirs that are used by loons. He has been working with the power companies to stop drawdown from mid-May to July. The sudden reduction of water level can isolate the nest, whether it is an island or shore location. With one- and two-foot reductions in level, the bird may have to crawl over land to get to and from the eggs, which can lead to nest failure.

The common loon has been studied most extensively on the southern fringe of its breeding range, which is in the northern United States. The edges of all organisms' ranges are areas of greatest environmental stress. They are tension zones, according to the old ecological texts. Here the birds are on the periphery of their acceptable habitat. Here their very existence might be marginal, and there are enough external factors to make observed behavior different than what might be considered normal within the center of the animals' range. For this reason it is interesting to note some of the conclusions Keith Yonge reached in his research on Hanson Lake in northern Saskatchewan, close to the center of the common loon's range.

On Hanson Lake, the birds arrived as soon as the ice was off, and they established territories immediately. This immediate establishment of territories is probably very important in the far North, where the ice-free season is short and there is little time to delay if chicks are to be full-grown before ice-in. Haste seems to be less important in the southern parts of the breeding range. In Minnesota, for example, the birds not only could nest later, but could spend more time in pair formation because of the longer ice-free season.

The loons of Hanson Lake preferred island nesting. All of the nests were constructed so that the incubating adult had an unobstructed view of the lake, and the concealment offered by vegetation was used to hide the nest from land rather than water.

There were chunks of moss in three-fourths of the nests, and this constituted 41 percent of their bulk. When it was available, the large aquatic grass phragmites, a tall grass that reaches up to ten feet above the water surface, was used as the primary nesting material. Sometimes called cane grass, this very strong-stemmed grass was used by Indians to weave drying baskets. In Minnesota, researchers have found that sphagnum moss is the most common nest material.

Loons use a wide variety of materials in nests. In 1985, Paul Valley was watching loons on the Whitefish Lake chain in Minnesota and observed one loon dive to the lake bottom, where it retrieved some muck that it tossed over its back toward the nest. The mate then took the muck and threw it on the nest with another toss of the head. Later, it was observed that while incubating, the loon would occasionally reach over the edge of the nest, grab some muck and toss it over its back onto the nest.

Some nests are just simple depressions in the sand. And in northern Maine, Paul Strong found a loon nest in a pile of freshwater mussel shells on a small island. The mussels had probably been an otter family's dinner.

Yonge also looked at the location of the common loon nest. In Minnesota, loons tend to locate their nests on the northwest shore of lakes, which prevents destruction by waves from the prevailing winds. In Yonge's study, the loons chose the side of the islands closest to a shore. On the extremely large Hanson Lake, this made sense; it left the wind with the least possible distance to travel over the water and create waves that might wash out the nest.

The red-throated loon also requires a nest site next to the water, which they can enter or exit with a quick slide. Their nest is a slight hollow, a depression just big enough to hold the bird's two eggs, and is normally lined with sphagnum, crowberry vine, and reindeer lichen.

The red-throated loon always seems to be just a little different from the other three species. They will nest on open spots where the surrounding vegetation is quite tall and on tarns (small lakes with little food available). In Finland, they are reported to be colonial nesters on some large islands.

Built-up nests (those started in water and constructed to rise above the water level) seem to be more common among red-throated loons than for the other loons. Davis found one built-up nest that was sixty centimeters in diameter at its base and narrowed to twenty centimeters above water. These nests take considerably more energy than the conventional bowl nests and must offer some advantages to support their common use. The most obvious advantage is that the bird does not have to wait until the spring high water subsides before it can nest in a particular area. In Davis's study there were forty-six built-up and forty-seven depression nests.

Like the common loon, the Pacific will reuse old nest territories. They will use much larger lakes than the red-throated, a choice that fits not only the food needs but also the defense abilities of both birds. The heavier Pacific loon is a better diver and prefers deep lakes. The lighter weight red-throated has greater surface agility and, therefore, is at a distinct advantage on the shallower ponds. The two species are not compatible. The Pacific loon will react with greater aggres-

Nests are built along the water's edge, which can make them very vulnerable to water level fluctuations and waves from passing boats. (P. Roberts)

Nearby aquatic vegetation is used to construct a nest or add to one already existing. (P. Roberts)

sion to a red-throated than to another Pacific.

The yellow-billed loon is a solitary nester similar to the common loon. One observer in Alaska wrote that the nests looked like the loon had cut the turf and turned it over like a piece of sod.

Life revolves around the nest. It is the anchor point for the loon's territorial displays and threats. It contains the future of the species.

MATING

Mating is the most difficult common loon behavior to observe. (In human terms, we may not find this so startling!) Some researchers, after much field effort, had to write that copulation might have occurred at night, because they were unable to observe the actual mating of the birds.

Two observers have attempted to fill this gap in our knowledge. In 1960, William Southern, of Northern Illinois University, was making bird observations in Crex Meadows, a Wisconsin state wildlife refuge, when he noticed "what appeared to be a white-capped wave moving irregularly across the lake."

He was at Phantom Flowage, which has a road along nearly one-half of its shoreline and affords the observer many good vantage points. Southern moved his vehicle closer, and as he did he found that there were two loon heads in the churning water. The birds were charging across the water with beating wings, one bird about fifteen to twenty feet behind the other.

The chase lasted for several hundred feet and terminated with both loons standing upright with stretched wings before making a synchronized dive. They reemerged and there was a series of short chases, with the lead bird appearing to tire at the end of each race. The chaser seemed to have more energy than the lead bird, and the chaser mounted the lead bird at the conclusion of their final chase. Both birds submerged, and it was forty seconds before they reappeared on the surface, with one bird still on top of the other.

At first, this was considered to be the elusive act of copulation. Ornithologists now believe it was territorial aggression, and one bird was trying to drown the other.

The second observation took place in Michigan in April 1968 by Jean Tate and James Tate, Jr., of the University of Michigan biological station. They put their scope on a loon that was poised upright on the water, with wings agitating the surface. About fifteen minutes after the opening display, two loons appeared from the marsh vegetation and swam to the open water. One of these loons rolled up on its left side in a preening position, and the second loon responded by swimming up to the preening bird. It was assumed that the preening bird was the female, because the approaching loon swam around and made contact with it.

The female submerged and the male rolled off to his left. When the female reappeared, the male rose, splashed water with his wings, and then let his breast return to the water with force. He submerged in front of the female with only head and neck above the water. She sat and watched.

The two birds engaged in this avian foreplay for five to seven minutes, then moved toward the northeast with the male in the lead. They came to a channel and the male let the female proceed. Partway up the channel the female climbed out of the water onto the wet vegetation and turned onto her left side. The male followed, slid his feet under her, and mated with her. The actual mating lasted about nine seconds.

The female remained on land for a minute, while the male returned to the water, held his neck and head stiffly, and dipped his bill. The two birds remained together constantly for the next thirty to forty minutes and began to pull nest material.

The red-throated loon has been known to construct a copulating platform near the water's edge. Margaret Petersen observed a pair of red-throated loons culminate their mating ritual with one bird crawling onto the land and pulling dead sedges around its side and breast. This loon repeated the action three times with her mate sitting in the water and patiently observing. The last time he joined her and copulation occurred. Unlike the other types of loon they engaged in no postcopulation display—or celebration, if we anthropomorphize.

The Pacific loon female, after a subtle movement near the shore, crawls on land with her tail toward the water and raises it to expose the white undertail feathers. While she is doing this, she presses her bill against her breast with the feathers on her neck and head depressed. If the male does not react quickly, she reenters the water. When the male does follow, she turns her tail sideways and copulation begins immediately, lasting about five seconds. As with the red-throated, there is no closing ritual.

EGGS

The eggs of all the species are large, drab, and only slightly mottled. In Rolph Davis's study, sixty-seven of ninety-one Pacific loon clutches and seventy-two of eighty-seven red-throated loon clutches were of two eggs. From these nests, Davis found that fifty-six of ninety Pacific chicks and thirty-nine of one hundred one red-throated survived. When the pairs hatched two eggs, the success rate of raising both chicks was negligible: eight of thirty-one Pacific and three of forty-two red-throated survived.

Common loons usually have two eggs to each nest, but there have been reports of one and three eggs. Audubon wrote that the common loon normally has three eggs in its nest, but researchers since then have found that this is far from the truth. These are extremely rare occurrences, and Audubon must have stumbled onto the exception in his quest for the normal. Another report of three eggs was made in 1920 by an observer in Alberta, who found two nests out of nineteen with three eggs.

Yonge's Saskatchewan study found that the common loon in the North has its peak laying period sev-

Observation of loons mating is very rare. Peter Roberts photographed this pair in June 1985 at a lake in northern Minnesota.

After copulation, the male rested momentarily beside the female. (P. Roberts)

Soon after copulation, both birds leave the nest. (P. Roberts)

en to eleven days after ice-off on the lakes; the peak period in Minnesota came four weeks after ice-off. In Iceland similar statistics were found. This all makes sense when we look at how much later the ice comes off on the far northern lakes—and even more important, how early the ice comes back on.

Yonge found that out of 424 eggs laid, there was a successful hatch of 38 percent. He also points out that the average time for incubation on Lake Hanson was three days less than that established for U.S. birds by Olson, Marshall, Bent, McIntyre, and Palmer.

The eggs consume the energy of all of the mated loons. For almost all of the time during their nearly month-long incubation, one of the two birds is out of the water and on the nest. In order to withstand the rigors of the incubating period, Pacific loons have to arrive at the nest site with an accumulation of fat. By the time of incubation, the female is as much as 28 percent below her arrival weight. The female then takes two weeks to recuperate while the male sits on the nest and rarely leaves the egg. The female relieves the male for the last two weeks. The common loon has a less strenuous rotation period, working in short shifts.

It is a dangerous time for the adult, although Johnson and Johnson's description of the red-throated loon in a 1935 issue of the *Wilson Bulletin* gives a more relaxed view of the effort. "Once settled to its liking, the bird sat quietly, even dozing now and then; caught a passing fly in its bill or picked at its wings and back."

The common loon's eggs look very much like the eggs of other loons. The most common number is two eggs per nest. (P. Roberts)

PREDATION

Predators on the four loon species vary. The Pacific loon is bothered by glaucous gulls, jaegers, red fox, and Arctic fox. In years when the cycle for avian and mammalian predators is high and the vole population is low, the Pacific loon can be totally unsuccessful at hatching eggs. The timing of the cackling goose hatching is also a factor for the Pacific loon, because jaegers and gulls often switch to the loon eggs after the goose eggs have hatched. In years when the predator cycles are low, the Pacific loon can nest on the mainland with success comparable to an island nest site.

In the common loon's large range, there is a variation in predators from one region to another. In the far North, mink replace the striped skunk and raccoon as the primary terrestrial mammalian predators.

Loons are affected by home owners who like to feed raccoons. This feeding sustains an abnormally high population of raccoons, efficient predators who do not restrict their diets to the free handouts.

THE LOON FAMILY

Loons are extremely protective and caring toward their young. This behavior is instinctively produced to allow the greatest success for the survival of their species. Even behavior that to human observers may seem unusually cold and cruel probably serves as a benefit to the species.

Nonetheless, people will always react tenderly to the sight of a downy black loon chick being carried on the back of its parent. People who own summer lake homes will keep their fingers crossed and scan the water closely to catch a glimpse of their resident loon family. They will go to great trouble to defend and protect "their" loons, so that when they pack up and leave the cabin on Labor Day, they can leave feeling confident that the young have grown to sufficient size to fly away. This year's success will mean another summer of loons the following year.

After courtship, nest building, and copulation, the long period of incubation begins. This period averages about thirty days. Eggs are laid at intervals, and they hatch at different times, in the same sequence that they were laid. Hatching intervals can range from as few as 6 hours to as many as 30 hours, with the average being 17.3. As the time for hatching nears, sounds can be heard coming from inside the shells. Vocal communication between the chicks while still in the shell is known to accelerate the growth of the younger embryo and lead to more synchronous hatching. If two eggs hatch within 12 hours of one another, both chicks generally leave the nest at the same time; otherwise the first-hatched chick, as soon as its feathers have dried, leaves the nest to be cared for by the other parent.

After emerging from the shell, the chick is an unsightly little creature, with wet black feathers plastered against its oddly shaped body. In a few short hours, though, the feathers dry and the chick is trans-

An adult loon climbs onto the nest. The pair shares incubating responsibilities. (D. Cox)

Incubation lasts about thirty days. For 99% of that time, one of the two loons is on the nest. (D. Cox)

During much of the incubation process, parent loons rotate the eggs. People are not the only ones bothered by black flies, as evidenced by this photo. (P. Roberts)

formed into a thoroughly fetching little ball of black fluff. In common loons, the feathers range from black to blackish brown on top, blending to a more greyish color on the throat, upper breast, and flanks. The belly and lower breast are white, while the legs and feet are shades of black and grey.

It is nearly impossible to observe the hatching of a loon chick in the wild, but people have observed captive chicks hatch. William Beebe, a curator of ornithology in New York, watched one such occurrence in 1903. After the hatching, he noticed that the downy plumes were sheathed in a fine tissue. After an hour or so, this began to split at the tip. Three hours later, the chick was covered with tiny, fluffy, long-stemmed down. The chick he observed was restless and rolled about, an action that seemed to help remove the sheaths from the down. Whether the chick does this on the nest or whether the parents assist in removal is unknown. The appearance of the chick's down reminded Beebe of beaver's or otter's fur.

Because the older chick has generally been off the nest for some period of time (as much as a full day in red-throated loons) before the second chick hatches, the older weighs more and is stronger than its sibling. Chicks weigh between 77 and 99 grams (2.75 to 3.5 ounces) at hatch. The older chick may weigh as much as 6 to 7 grams (1/4 ounce) more by the time its sibling has hatched, due to the food it has been fed by the other parent. One of the less happy realities of loon life is that the second chick's chances of survival are significantly lower than the first chick's. Parental behavior and sibling competition strongly favor the older chick, who appears to lead the life of a much-favored older child.

Until recently, there has been little documentation on sibling rivalry among loons. In the last few years, more research has shown that young loons do in fact develop a dominance hierarchy. Usually within the first three days that the two loons are on the water together, pecking fights can be observed. Either one may initiate the pecking, but the older and stronger one has a better chance of inflicting a more painful "punch."

Wildlife photographer Peter Roberts observed a dramatic demonstration of this kind of conflict while filming a loon family on Ten Mile Lake in Minnesota. Both adult loons were in the water with the older chick, and they were calling to the second-hatched chick, which was only hours old, to come into the water. After some coaxing, it left the nest and the other three loons swam over to it. Immediately on meeting, the two little loons engaged in a violent pecking fight. They rolled about in the water, reared up and flapped their wings, and pecked at each other's heads until the younger chick finally put his head under water in an act of submission. The older chick stopped pecking and turned its back. As soon as it did this, the younger chick attacked and the fight began anew. Again, it only ended after the younger chick behaved submissively. The parent loons swam and dove nearby during

Soon after a chick hatches, the parent removes the eggshell remains from the nest. This probably removes scent that could attract predators. (P. Roberts)

43

Within a few hours after hatching, the loon chick is covered with fluffy, coal black, downy feathers. (P. Roberts)

Sometimes loon chicks need coaxing from the parents to leave the nest. (P. Roberts)

the fight, but did not interfere in any way. The subordinate chick finally accepted its fate, and subsequently, the older sibling always fed first. Welcome to the world!

Gary Dulin, a researcher from the University of Minnesota, from 1984 to 1986 observed young loons engaged in this sort of activity. He found that fights lasted only a few seconds and occurred only three or four times a day, but were enough to establish a strong dominance in the older chick. Once that dominance is established, it needs little reinforcement.

If a parent arrives with food and the chicks race to it, the stronger one gets there first and the younger hangs back in order to avoid an attack. If the younger one does compete for food with its sibling, it feels the hard point of a beak on its head. The second chick ends up feeding only after the first chick is satiated. Gary Dulin observed that in the first two weeks together, parent loons distributed food evenly between the two chicks, but by the third week, the older chick began to dominate the feedings, receiving as much as 60 to 70 percent of the food presented during a day. As time went on, the subordinate chick spent less and less time with the family group and finally disappeared. This usually happened sometime between the third and sixth week.

An earlier study by Davis showed that starvation was the main factor contributing to chick mortality among Pacific and red-throated loons. Here again, competition between the siblings, and parental discrimination, meant the first-born chick prospered at the expense of the second.

The second chick, because it is not as big as the first to begin with and continues to lag behind in growth, is more susceptible to exposure and predation. In one study, a family of loons was observed reacting to an intruder. The parents sent the chicks to shore for safety. The intruder remained, but the parents called the chicks back. After only one returned they swam away, even though the other chick could be heard calling. It is not known whether it was the older or younger chick that returned first to the parents, but again, the older, stronger chick would have been the most likely.

Much of the behavior of a loon family with two chicks indicates that the younger one is certainly at a competitive disadvantage—and in the scheme of nature, expendable. Dulin found that a second chick was more likely to survive if adults delivered a variety of different-sized food items. The older chick may refuse larger fish and crayfish, which the younger one may accept and successfully swallow. In this way, both receive equal amounts of food by weight, even though the older one receives more of the smaller, easily swallowed food.

The long-term success of the species favors a dominance hierarchy system such as this. If food supply is adequate and the parent loons have time to deliver enough food to the chicks, both survive. If, however, it is a bad year for the food supply, at least the dominant chick survives. A lack of dominance would mean that both chicks would compete evenly for less food, and probably both would die.

Parent loons don't practice favoritism; they do not seem to recognize a difference between one chick and another. They simply respond to the most demanding and accessible chick. Because of the distances between nurseries, the limited movement of chicks, and strong territorial defense, there has been little need for loons to develop chick recognition. For stray chicks to end up in the wrong territory has been unlikely. This lack of ability to identify their own chicks is most clearly demonstrated in examples of loons that have become "foster" or "adoptive" parents.

In 1984, in northern Maine, a family of loons was observed with three chicks, although the nest had been seen earlier containing only two eggs. It is believed that the extra chick came from a neighboring territory and either was blown across the lake or followed adults during a territorial dispute. Nests in the neighboring loon territories had also contained two eggs, and after the eggs hatched, the various families were observed with either one or two chicks. When the family with the three chicks was seen, other families had reduced numbers of chicks.

People have introduced loon chicks to nests or territories and they have been accepted. One example of this occurred in June 1980 in Vilas County, Wisconsin. Some people brought a loon chick about ten days old into Aqualand Animal Park. Even though the chick was surviving on minnows at the park, the staff knew that its best chance for survival was to be reared by a pair of loons with chicks of similar age.

A loon family was found nearby, and Ron Eckstein, from the Wisconsin DNR in Rhinelander, took the chick in a motorboat and approached within 100 feet of the two adults and one chick. One of the parents responded in typical threat fashion, while the other swam with the chick toward shore. Ron tossed the chick into the water, toward the loon that was displaying. The chick turned and swam back to the boat. Ron threw it back two more times before it spotted the adult and swam toward it. The adult stopped its display, swam next to the chick and escorted it away from the boat and toward shore. Within a minute, the chick was riding on the adult's back. The two adults and two chicks met at the shoreline, and an extended family was formed. Three weeks later, Ron observed the family again. Both chicks had doubled in size; one was larger than the other, but both appeared healthy and strong. The adults were seen feeding both chicks.

The fact that loons will accept young other than their own may prove to be an effective management technique in areas where loon productivity is low and habitat is favorable.

The first two weeks of life are the most danger-ridden for the loon chick. The highest mortality occurs in the first four days. If a chick can survive to three weeks of age, its chances of reaching fledging age are very good. Just prior to hatching, and after hatching but before they get into the water, the young are susceptible to predation by mammals, especially raccoons, fox, and mink. Gulls will also attack the nest. Once the chick is in the water, death can come from the sky or the depths below. Snapping turtles and northern pike are known to take small waterfowl. This is believed to be one of the reasons why very young chicks spend so many hours—some say as much as 50 to 65 percent of their first two weeks—riding on the backs of the adults. Back riding may also be a means of warming a wet, cold chick or assisting one that has become exhausted.

To do this an adult loon partially submerges itself so that the little loon can climb aboard. To disembark its passenger, the adult rises and shakes its feathers or partially submerges again. The sight of a chick riding "piggyback" on an adult loon is probably *the* most heartwarming sight for a loon lover.

Wheeling overhead, herring gulls scan the water for easy pickings. A week-old loon chick can be scooped up off the water in a flash. Here is a situation where a second chick is at a distinct disadvantage. While the parents are responding to a threat to one chick, the other may drift away and become an easier target for the marauding gull. In recent years, with the successful return of eagles to northern lakes, there have been more reports of these birds harassing loon chicks on the water.

Other loons invading a territory can threaten and kill chicks, and large waves can hopelessly separate them from their parents. Because there are so many dangers to the young loons, the parents are quick to respond in strong measure when a threat appears. Loon chicks grow quickly, not only to defend themselves against attack but also to ensure their chances of being able to leave the lakes in the fall before freeze-up occurs.

Swimming ability, peering, feeding, rearing up, wing flapping, and preening are all well developed in the first two days of a loon's life. Attempts to dive occur soon after the chicks get into the water, but they are less capable in this area, popping up like a cork until their legs become stronger and can push their buoyant bodies below the surface. It may be close to two weeks before their diving ability is well developed.

In the first few days of life, loon chicks are kept very near the parents. At this time, generally just one parent dives for food, while the other stays near the chick. A loon does not regurgitate food to its young, but rather carries food to them crosswise in its bill. The adult lowers its head and extends it neck until the chick can reach the fish. If the chick is hungry, it will grasp it. Human parents know that sometimes it takes great effort to interest a human baby in its food. We go to great lengths to turn a spoonful of squash into an airplane flying around in front of the baby's face. Parent loons have a similar tactic. A parent tries to entice the chick to feed by moving its head from side to side, so that the food passes close to the chick's head. This may continue for some minutes, with the fish being dipped frequently in the water before being presented to the chick.

After the chick grasps the fish crosswise in its mandible, it shifts it, by a series of head jerks along with biting action, until the head of the fish is in position to be swallowed first. Smaller fish are naturally easier to shift and swallow, but as the chick gets bigger, the parents present larger fish.

Sometimes the parents appear to test the young bird with a fish that is more than it can easily handle. Wildlife photographers Jan and Des Bartlett were filming red-throated loons in a remote area of the Northwest Territories in Canada when they watched one chick struggle with an extra-large fish. While the chick tried to swallow it headfirst, the parent continued to hold on to the other end. The chick had to kick its feet furiously in order to keep above water during the attempt. After the chick finally got most of the fish down, a portion of the tail protruded from its beak for an hour or longer—a truly good example of "more than a mouthful."

Adult loons also occasionally catch a fish too large to swallow. Paul Strong watched one adult loon in Maine struggle with a white sucker about fifteen inches long for five minutes before it finally got the fish partially swallowed. Like the chick, it swam around with the fish's tail hanging out of its mouth for many minutes.

The different species of loons provide their young with different types of food. Young Pacific loons are

Chicks spend 50 to 65% of their first two weeks riding on the adults' backs. The parent partially submerges itself so the chick can climb aboard. (P. Roberts)

Research indicates a dominance hierarchy among loon chicks. The first-hatched chick has a definite advantage in size and strength. (P. Roberts)

fed small invertebrate prey, one at a time, as well as small freshwater fish. Red-throated loons nest on very small lakes near coastal regions, so the parents have to leave the natal lake and make feeding flights to the sea. Their young are fed herring, sea perch, sand launce, and cod. There may be many reasons why red-throated loons go to such great trouble and distance to feed their chicks. The lakes may be too small to support an adequate supply of fresh fish. If there are fish in the lake, the reduced amount of water is likely to mean an increased chance of fish being infected with parasites that could infect the loons. Finally, the marine fish contain higher levels of minerals and vitamins than the freshwater fish.

Perch is the most frequently identified food given to common loon young, but it is difficult to observe closely enough and long enough to identify all the food being fed. Studies of stomach contents of adult loons have shown large amounts of perch and minnows, followed by suckers, trout, and bullhead. Nonfish remains were dominated by crayfish. Leeches have been found in the digestive track in sufficient numbers to indicate that they are an important food item. Most research indicates that loons are adaptive to their particular environment and make use of the most abundant and easily caught prey, which in most cases is perch.

Paul Strong, in his study of loon habitat, found that for the early rearing of the chicks, loons preferred shallow-water areas close to land, protected from prevailing winds and heavy wave action. This may have something to do with food availability, since yellow perch and minnows are most abundant in shallow water. It also may allow the chicks to develop early foraging skills.

Most common loons nest on lakes that have provided them with sufficient food to raise young in years past. With serious changes in air quality, namely acid rain, some loons have nested on traditional lakes but have been forced to go elsewhere to find food for their young. In July 1984, Karl Parker, of the Department of Environmental and Forest Biology, in South Hamilton County of New York observed common loons flying from one lake to another with fish in their bills. The two lakes were two kilometers apart. The smaller lake, where the loons had nested, was almost devoid of fish due to acid rain. The larger lake yielded limited numbers of three species of fish.

Apparently, the fish at the smaller lake were not enough to satisfy the food needs of the young, and the adults had begun flying to the larger lake to supplement the food supply. Whenever adult loons have to fly to find food, not only are they expending extra energy of their own, but they are leaving the young open to predation. Red-throated loons, which commonly practice this type of system, rarely raise more than one chick a year, and they do this in areas with less predation, since the aquatic environment is void of predators large enough to eat their young.

As the chicks grow older, both parents feed them,

48

and the entire family begins to forage farther from shore. By the third week, the parent will drop an injured fish in front of a chick, who then retrieves it. In this way, chicks may learn to recognize patterns of swimming by fish that are easier to catch. Perch, for instance, swim in an erratic zigzag when chased. Any pursued and tiring fish may turn more frequently, attracting the bird's attention and exposing itself to attack. When swimming fast underwater, the loon is able to use its leg like a brake, sticking it out and pivoting quickly enough to strike with its bill at a fish making a dodging manuever. Smaller fish are captured more frequently because they can't achieve the burst of great speed that larger fish use for escape.

By eight weeks of age, young loons are almost fully feathered, and their legs and feet are almost the size of an adult's, leading to greater ability in chasing and capturing prey. The parents go off to feed for longer periods, leaving the chicks to forage for themselves. When the parents return, they generally offer food to the young. At eleven weeks, the young will still beg for food from their parents, even though they feed independently most of the day.

To reach the age of fledging requires not only a little luck but also much concentrated protective effort on the part of the loon parents. From the outset the young are closely guarded. When the chicks aren't back riding in the early days, they are swimming between the two parents. If one chick falls behind, the parents vocally encourage it to catch up; if that fails,

one or both parents drop back to accompany it. Loons learn at a very early age how to hide when danger threatens. Responding to some means of communication from the adults, the chicks dive and head for the shoreline.

When threatened, young red-throated loons dive to the bottom of a small pond and stir up the mud with their feet, then turn back into the muddy water to be lost from sight. They pop up for air, dive again, and continue to stir up the sediment until the entire pond is murky and they can hide along the shore under a bank of aquatic vegetation.

When danger threatens their chicks, parent loons try to create diversionary activity to distract the intruder. The most dramatic display is the penguin dance, described in Chapter 4. This display has been observed even when the eggs have been lost, and it may be that it is a mechanical reaction during a particular physiological stage of the reproductive process and is produced automatically when the nesting territory is invaded. If necessary, the adult loons will physically attack in defense of their young. They have been known to stab at the eyes of a predator, including young polar bears.

Another wildlife photography team had a very close and painful encounter with a loon family they were trying to film underwater. Sharon and Kip Taylor wanted to film two-day-old loon chicks diving and catching food. Every time Kip, the scuba-diving cameraman, swam close to the chick, one parent

Loon chicks continue to beg for food from their parents long after they are capable of catching their own fish. (P. Roberts)

would go into threat displays to lure him away. The other parent would attack, aiming its beak at the cameraman's goggles. The chick lost its fear and even settled momentarily on his submerged shoulder. This, however, enraged the adult loon even more, and Kip learned just how hard and dangerous a loon's beak can be, after it struck his head and drew blood.

Not all responses to threats are as vehement or violent. It depends on the closeness of the threat to the young and the age of the chicks. A pair of loons may choose to stay with their young and remain silent if a canoe is seen some distance away.

This past August we spent a day canoeing in the Boundary Waters and had just portaged over to Hook Lake. We were drifting with the wind when up ahead we spotted two dark heads on the water. Binoculars showed two adult loons and a good-sized juvenile a short distance behind them. The adults spotted us and began to cast frequent glances over their left sides. We heard no sounds, but they let Junior know they were concerned. He drew close and one adult dove out of sight. Moments later, a tremolo call came from across the lake, behind and to our right. The old decoy ploy. As we looked in that direction, the juvenile slipped away. The two adults tremoloed back and forth, and the wind continued to push us toward the remaining adult, who finally dove and came up behind us. Meanwhile, the young loon had made its way, without our noticing, over to the parent that had left first. We had witnessed the extreme wariness and caution of parent loons—even for almost fully grown young.

As the young continue to grow and become more capable of defending themselves, the loon family may begin to engage in activities that to us may look like fun and games. In 1892, Dr. P. L. Hatch of Minnesota wrote about a family of loons engaged in "matutinal jollifications"—translated from Webster's to mean "early morning revelry." Dr. Hatch went on to describe how the loon family fell into a line: "Side by side and lifting their wings simultaneously, they start off in a footrace on the water . . . running with incredible speed a full quarter of a mile without lowering their wings or pausing for an instant, wheel around in a short circle . . . and retrace their course to the place of starting. This race, after a moment's pause, is repeated over and over again with unabated zest, until by some undiscoverable signal it ceases as suddenly as it began."

Summer wanes and the young loons are fully feathered and ready for flight—some say as young as seven to eight weeks, and most certainly by ten weeks—but flight in the nesting territory is rare, even for the adults. As late as ten to thirteen weeks into the chicks' lives, the parents may still offer fish to their well-grown offspring. But the day is fast drawing near when the parents, one at a time, feel the pull of migration and leave.

With their parents gone, the young loons leave the nesting territories behind, move about, and associate with other recently orphaned adolescents. There are still some fine autumn days left in the year, but the temperature and leaves are falling quickly. How does the young loon learn to lift itself from the water into the highways of the sky? It probably comes as a surprise. Maybe a group of juveniles engage in some more "matutinal jollifications" and instead of settling back into the familiar water, they find themselves moving up and away from their comrades below. A few sweeps around their birthplace and they're gone—another summer success.

(P. Roberts)

50

Loons react aggressively to defend their territory. This can result in injuries. Photographer Peter Roberts once observed a loon and a beaver in a violent confrontation. A broken beak would not be a surprising result. (P. Roberts)

LOON AGGRESSION

Across a small lake fringed in tamarack and spruce, a mallard hen swam with nine ducklings. They were still in their down fuzzball stage, wandering a few feet, then scrambling back in a frenzy of flippers and peeps. Suddenly, a duckling disappeared. The family moved on.

Another rose from the water, then settled back, dead. The scene was repeated with still another duckling. The ducks sensed something, and fear spread. The threat was from below—a turtle? No, too many young, too much distance between deaths, too fast. A northern? No, too many dead. The count continued to mount, and by the time the mallard got to the safety of shallow water on the far shore, she had only two ducklings left.

On the same lake, a game farmer had a mandarin duck drake escape from one of his pens. He grabbed his canoe and set out to recapture the bird, but as he approached the drake, it suddenly rose out of the water and then collapsed on its side. He picked it up. The bird was dead, with a hole that came up from below and behind. The death blow pierced the vital organs.

With female teal nesting in a game farm box, the males drifted around the perimeter of their nest territory. Because they detected no apparent threat, they relaxed and slept in the warmth of the sun. Suddenly, one collapsed—dead from an underwater attack.

Isolated experiences? A Loch Ness monster? What does this have to do with loons? Do they suffer these attacks too? Yes, they do—but more important, they are the attackers.

Nature is not mild, meek, and filled with peace. Everything is eaten by something else. Competition is not a game, but survival. The loon kills to eat and kills to maintain its territory. It is agressive and powerful and it has survived since the Paleocene.

Mark Sperry, of the Minnesota DNR, observed two separate attacks on duck broods by loons. During one episode, two loons attacked a female goldeneye and her seven one-week-old ducklings. The loon attacked from underwater. The ducklings dispersed and dove while the adult called and flapped on the surface. A loon picked one duckling up in its bill, flung it into the air and dove after another. Two ducklings were killed in this attack. Other goldeneye and ring-necked duck mortalities were reported as well. The common denominator in all these deaths was an attack from below and a puncture through the abdomen.

The report also includes incidents of adult mortality in goldeneyes. There is even one report of a loon killing an adult Canada goose.

The result of these attacks can be the elimination of a nest or a brood. Either way, the loon is decreasing competition and increasing the potential for survival of its young.

The loon is vulnerable on land for the thirty days of incubation. The young are flightless on the lake for two months, and the adults are flightless during their winter molt. They can't fly away from trouble, so they must confront it.

It is hard to see how a dabbling duck, such as a mallard, can be competition, but we have to assume that the loon cannot tell a dabbler from a diver. Game farmers resent the loon for its aggression, just as many commercial fishermen resented it for the fish it took. The question is, can we accept it as something other than a stuffed toy with a shiny black beak and red eyes? Can we see it as an animal that has characteristics both interesting and frustrating, and still cherish it as part of the northern lake country wilderness? Is its survival dependent on its fulfilling our human expectations, or can we accept it as a complex part of our northern ecology?

The young loon's feet and legs develop more quickly than do the wings. By eight weeks of age, the chick's feet and legs are almost the same size as the adult's. (P. Roberts)

LEGS AND WINGS

If the loon wanted to use its legs for walking, it would have to walk upright like a human or a chimp. It is impossible, in terms of physics, for a fulcrum to be placed where the loon's legs are and the body to be held up off the ground—unless the tail feathers are made of lead.

On land, the hindquarters are raised and the bird furrows like a wheelbarrow. In *Life Histories of North American Diving Birds*, Bent includes a report of young birds going across the land much more easily and rapidly than the adult. The reporter William Beebe described the young as moving with froglike bounds.

The loon's legs are located near the tail, for diving and swimming, not for launching or strolling. The bird's entire body is made for the water. The loon can control its buoyancy to float fully immersed or with most of its body on the surface. But what the loon does best is dive.

With a sudden plunge of the head, the large, sharp beak leads the way as the loon dives into the depths. The body is streamlined, torpedo-like, the head is large, the neck strong. The legs push the body through the water with hard strokes and minimum drag. The feet fold up, leaving a cutting edge to move forward with each individual stroke. At the point of forward stroke, the foot unfolds and the three large front toes command a full webbing that allows the bird to overtake the fish it is chasing.

The wings are not like other birds'. They look more like fins than the graceful, soft-feathered appendages that we expect. Audubon reported that the loon used its wings to swim through the water and that the bird's speed was due to this extra stroke. Modern scientists discount this idea. The wings are used in some parts of the swim, but more for controlling direction and making turns than for speed.

The red-throated loon can almost spring from the water to the air like a mallard, but the common loon requires up to a quarter mile, or more, to get airborne. The head rises, the wings flap, the legs churn. The loon flies/runs across the lake in a low-altitude flight, leaving a trailing wake. Then the body begins to lift, the head and the chest thrust forward, the tail feathers emerge from the water, the feet slap the surface in quick panicky steps, water splashes from each foot— the bird can feel the moment of lift approaching. It moves faster, the effort is frantic, the wings catch air, the feet lift off the surface, the body gets horizontal to the surface and the bird is flying. Just watching exhausts the observer.

In the air the feet become efficient tools of flight. The loon, with its hunchbacked silhouette, can make long, fast journeys toward the sea. In March 1948, a bird-watching doctor from Boston was flying a Piper Cub near Charlotte, North Carolina, when he noticed a common loon flying at about 1200 feet. He decided to follow the loon, and turned his plane to track it. After a shallow dive, the bird resumed its flight pattern and maintained a speed of eighty to one hundred miles per hour. In flight the loon uses a combination of legs and wings, just as it does in the water. This time, the feet stick out behind the bird and make up for the small tail.

A loon can't take off if it isn't on water or if the water surface is too short for a running start. At least, they aren't supposed to be able to fly from land—this is the rule, but like all such, it has exceptions.

The Minnesota Department of Natural Resources received a report from the Brainerd area of an unusual sighting. On Highway 371 just north of Brainerd, a common loon adult was observed trying to cross a four-lane highway with two downy chicks. The person who reported the event could hardly believe his eyes, but could not resist stopping to assist. He stopped his car, flagged down the oncoming traffic, picked up the two chicks, and carried them across the road. The adult was not about to be assisted and showed signs of distress. It started to flap its wings and vocalize. For about 300 feet, the length of a football field, the loon ran/flapped across the grass in the center median. It became airborne with sufficient altitude to clear a line of shrubs ten to fifteen feet high. It flew to the lake it had been heading for, made a number of calls from the water, and was soon rejoined by the released chicks.

When the DNR official investigated this unusual observation, he concluded that the adult must have nested on a seven-acre pond on one side of the highway and then decided to move the young over a 250-foot distance to a 6,178-acre lake.

This isn't the only record of the land travels of loons. In another area near Brainerd, a boy found a loon chick about 250 feet from water, bounding through the forest. The sight of a loon hopping like a frog in the forest is a strange one, and the boy's curiosity was piqued. He picked up the downy black chick and took it home, where he asked his mother what he should do with the young bird. She suggested that he release it in the lake in front of their house because an adult had been swimming back and forth along the beach, uttering a mournful wail, for the past day and a half.

In the lake, the chick began to drink water rapidly to make up for the dehydration that had taken place on the land. Then the young bird began to mew in a soft, almost inaudible voice. The adult that had been patrolling the lake heard the call and immediately came to investigate. When the two birds came into visual contact the adult rose, flapped its wings, and vocalized with its neck stretched vertically. Then it settled down, submerged, and came up with fish that it fed to the young. The nearest other body of water to this place of reunion was about one-half mile away. The loon adult must have flown and then tried to call its young to it.

In one report at Lake Itasca, the headwaters for the Mississippi River, a loon chick was observed crossing the land barrier between Desoto and Mangose lakes, a distance of twenty yards. Disturbance caused by a lowered water level initiated the movement.

In the area near Baldwin, Wisconsin, loons were seen crossing the road near Oakridge Lake on three consecutive nights. It is hard to understand why the loons would have been on land for more than one crossing, but on the third night the walking stopped when one of the chicks was struck by a car. It may have been the only road-killed loon chick in history.

There are still more observations of hiking loons, traveling from small ponds to big lakes. The Minocqua area in Wisconsin and the Seney Wildlife Refuge in the Upper Peninsula of Michigan have recent reports of walking loons.

The most curious event of all, however, came in 1986, on Highway 371 north of Brainerd, Minnesota, when an adult loon and two chicks tried to cross the four-lane road. A man went to help and the adult took off from land. Sound familiar? This was three years after the first incident, and in the same location.

The loon's legs are set very far back on the body, making it awkward on land, but an excellent diver. (P. Roberts)

The common loon requires more than a quarter mile to become airborne. Running across the surface, it leaves "splashprints" in its wake. (P. Roberts)

The loon in flight has a characteristic hunchbacked silhouette. (P. Roberts)

As parenting responsibilities end, loons gather into premigratory flocks. Photographer Peter Roberts observed these three loons engaged in an early morning ritual.

FLOCKING AND MIGRATING

Have you ever canoed on a large lake and encountered a concentration of loons? On Cache Bay of Saganaga Lake on the Canadian border, I paddled into a flock of more than one hundred birds in early September. There were gulls and mergansers on the lake as well, but the common loon dominated the waters.

They formed large strings that radiated into the smaller divisions of the bay, but they seemed to have no purpose in their behavior. The birds weren't fishing, calling, or displaying. Occasionally one bird would rise and stretch its wings, but they seemed content to merely drift and avoid my canoe. I wondered about this fall phenomenon for a long time, but I never found an explanation for it.

The loon engages in many activities that scientists and naturalists are uncertain about, activities that we can observe with some frequency but can't analyze. The more we study these animals, the more complex they become. It's nice to have these mysteries left in life.

Migration is one of those events that we struggle to explain in all birds. With the loon we add the irregular flocking behavior to the mystery, and we hazard a few guesses as to why the birds might congregate at various lakes and times. But we don't know the answer.

Loon migration is not known as a flock activity. It is described as an irregular movement of singles and pairs, with the adults preceding the young to the winter ocean grounds. The young loons must decide when they must leave to avoid freeze-up. Think of how complex this is behaviorally. They have never even seen a lake freeze up. In their lives, they have only seen summer on their natal lake, yet they must predict and avoid the thrusts of winter to survive. As we show in another essay, they don't always make the proper decision. Imagine the challenge ahead for the young who must travel to oceans they have never seen, with no adults to guide them.

While loon migration is normally too sporadic to observe with regularity, Rick Julian, of the Fish and Wildlife Service, reports that in the Red Lake Manage-ment Area of northwestern Minnesota, he observed almost a steady stream of migrants at a corner north of Fourtown and south of Warroad two years in a row (1972 and 1973). The birds were moving northwest each April that they were seen. Red Lakes are southeast of this spot and Lake of the Woods is northeast; both are extremely large bodies of water and have many resident summer loons.

At Whitefish Point in Michigan in 1981, David Ewert conducted a count of migrating loons over Lake Superior. From April 25 to June 8, there were 225 hours of observations, which indicated that the loons moved in small groups from 7 to 8 A.M.

In the spring Lake Superior may still have ice packs, although most will be off by early May. For this reason, Lakes Huron and Michigan serve as a staging area until the ice is off on the northern waters. St. Marys River between Huron and Superior may be a major movement corridor for the common loon.

The migrant loons observed were primarily in pairs; any larger groups were relatively loose aggregations of birds, not the structured flocks that we see in geese and other waterfowl. There were many groups of three, a few groups of four and six, and one group each of eight, nine, ten, and eleven loons.

In northern parts of their range, common loons must be paired up when they arrive in order to initiate quick nesting. Yonge points out that pair bonding appears to have been completed by the time the birds arrive. It is possible that some of the migratory flocking includes pair-bonding activities on resting lakes. The flocks are often more than one hundred individuals. These migratory flocks may develop as a staging activity to time arrival with ice-off.

In *Seabirds*, Peter Harrison says that the common loon has less of a tendency to flock than the red-throated and Arctic loons, but that they gather in large flocks on the Great Lakes. There are many recordings of summer flocks of common loons that seem to contradict this statement.

59

A report from Winnipeg's environmental agency in 1972 summarized reports from Lake Athapapuskow, Wildnest Lake, and Kississing Lake that include flocks of one to two hundred in June and July. The flocks would form and re-form daily, with individual birds coming in from many directions, and flock size reaching a peak around 3 P.M. Perhaps in this sense we can agree with Harrison that the flocks did not last, but reconvened. In the Flin Flon area there were regular reports of this flocking activity over a thirty-year period. From our data, we can conclude that this must be considered a regular activity.

In Minnesota, Sigurd T. Olson noted that groups of ten to thirty loons gathered regularly on the large lakes in canoe country. In addition to engaging in many social interactions, they formed what appeared to be fishing lines. Like pelicans, the loons would line up evenly spaced and move in a coordinated fashion across the lake.

On Hanson Lake, Yonge noted that broodless common loon adults were less common on their territories during the summer, and by August there was usually only one adult with the juveniles. This leaves all but the attentive parent available to form flocks.

In northern Saskatchewan, the adult birds gather in flocks before departing on migration. There is usually a two- or three-day interval between the departures of the individuals of a mated pair.

Other loon species also engage in flocking. The Pacific loons that fail to breed join roving flocks that move from one lake to another and land in the territories of other unsuccessful birds. The birds then join in communal displays with up to twelve displaying at the same time. The group avoids territories of successful breeders. If a territorial bird shows sings of agitation and aggression, the flock leaves it alone. Many times, after a group display the territorial loon joins the roving band. This may be a way of mapping the breeding territory and gaining recognition of other individuals.

There are fewer flocks of red-throats, and they engage in aerial calls while in flying flocks rather than in aquatic displays.

In the fall migration, the Great Lakes are a common stopover spot and may even hold Pacific, red-throated, and common loons at the same time. There is a yellow-billed loon record for Lake Superior as well.

Mille Lacs is a very large lake in central Minnesota, with a fall abundance of tullibees and a late freeze-up. Occasionally sightings of large loon concentrations are recorded as late as mid-November on Mille Lacs. T. R. Campbell reported that "As far as we could see, clear to the horizon, there were loons everywhere, all flying straight east. . . . I would estimate that at least 500 loons passed through my viewing area between 7 A.M. and 9 A.M."

When we see it in the nesting territory, the common loon is a solitary or a family bird; we do not think of it as a flocking bird like a crow or a snow bunting. But the flock serves an important function for loons that are unsuccessful nesters, for those enroute to nesting territory, and for juveniles migrating to the sea. There is a collective wisdom in numbers, and the flock represents a pool of knowledge for the individual. Each season the potential for nesting success changes; those birds that pair up in the migratory flock, or those that learn from associations within a flock, are most apt to succeed when the opportunity arises.

Humans pride themselves on their collective wisdom, but loons demonstrate that we share with many other creatures the ability to learn from others. The big question is—who learns their lessons better?

WINTER LOONS

The northerner knows fall migration better than anyone who lives in the South. In southern areas, migration is an increase in the population; there are more kinds and greater numbers of birds, but the change is one of degree.

In the North, it is the beginning of a long absence, not addition but subtraction.   The loon is good to us—it stays as long as it can and it returns as quickly as possible. Perhaps that is why we love it so much—it truly is a hardy northerner. But we worry about our loon when it is gone. We hear about loons washing up on the Florida coastline, and we try to think of what the loon is doing in the salt water for so many months. We have learned that the young loon takes a three-year or longer hiatus in the Gulf and Atlantic before returning, a mature and experienced adult, to nest in the waters of our northern forests. But there are many questions that we still don't have answers to.

How does the loon survive there? How do these freshwater birds live on saltwater diets? Do they have a process for eliminating the excess salt from their bodies? Robert Storer, in Michigan, found that the loon does have salt glands, which are located in the fleshy part of the head above the nostrils. The salt is eliminated in a liquid form that drips out of the nostril and then flows out the grooves on the bill.

Loons' saltwater diet consists of cod, sea trout, herring, flounder, sculpin, surf fish, menhaden, and mackerel. Bernard King noted that they also eat crabs, both shore crabs and edible crabs. King occasionally observed a loon come to the surface gulping and shaking its head, as if it had swallowed a crab on the way, but most often the bird would come to the surface with the crab. It would then shake the crustacean and soften it with its bill before swallowing.

Judy McIntyre, who began her work in Minnesota and continues her research in the East, also observed the wintering common loon. She noted that the birds off Assateague Island, Virginia, would feed together for four to eight hours a day and then raft together at night. In the middle to late afternoon, the birds often stopped feeding and then preened or slept, drifting to the center of the cove in loose aggregations.

Feeding was particularly influenced by tidal movement. Less frequent during the most rapid tidal influx,

Loons do not migrate in flocks, but it is not unusual to see a pair flying together. (P. Roberts)

it peaked when the tide flow slowed down and then declined again at high tide. At high tide and between feeding periods, most of the loons just drifted. In the approximate six-hour period between tides, the peaks of feeding were at low tide and again three to four hours after low tide.

Tides influence loon behavior in other ways too. With the influx of tides are influxes of food species. The birds do not have to fly to other locations to feed; they have tremendous abundance throughout the tidal zone. They do not have to fly for safety; they can ride the tides in and out and dive and swim as far as they want. They are in a relatively safe environment, which lacks only the proper conditions for nesting.

The common loon does not molt before heading to the sea, so its feathers can be frayed and damaged by the time it reaches salt water. Loon wings are not very aerodynamic in design even when all the feathers are new and shapely. After numerous flights and dives plus the stress of migration, a loon's wing feathers are ready for replacement.

The replacement of feathers during molt takes more energy than the bird can afford while raising the young. There is too short a period between migrations for both nesting and molting. The replacement feathers take three to four weeks to develop. On the nest lake, this much time after the chicks are successfully raised would trap the loons in the lake ice. The loss of a single flight feather can make the loon flightless and helpless on the northern lakes. So loons generally molt in late winter. Only the red-throated loon replaces its feathers in the summer. (As we keep saying, the red-throated is an exception in almost every way.)

The young of all loon species replace their flight feathers (remiges) both summer and winter. They do not leave the salt water at this time of their lives, so they can afford the replacement costs.

On the winter ground, we observe many flightless birds enjoying the abundance and protection of the ocean. The birds protect smaller territories for their feeding and show more tolerance of other individuals than in the summer. But their winter behavior mimics the summer in some ways. For example, regardless of the tides, they still begin feeding just before dawn and end feeding after sunset. On the winter ground, they still need light for hunting; they are visual hunters, using eyesight for location and capture of prey. Another example is their flocking, which is similar to summer aggregations where the birds have social interactions but fish as individuals.

The wintering ground covers a wide variety of temperatures from the northern coasts to the Gulf. It appears that the availability of food is more important than a warm climate in the choice of wintering grounds. Loon feathers are structured in such a way that they literally zip together to protect the birds from cold and wetness. When the birds preen, they oil the feathers, and they cause the little barbs to interlock. With dry down next to the skin, the birds are very warm. They don't leave our nothern lakes because of the cold, but because of the ice.

Sigurd Olson once observed some loons swimming in what appeared to be a fishing line. They were evenly spaced and moving in a coordinated fashion, much like pelicans. (P. Roberts)

These loons are peering into the water, apparently watching other loons swimming below — notice the ripples on the surface, caused by the submerged loons. (P. Roberts)

(P. Roberts)

POISON IN THE WATER

LETHAL RAIN

A rainy, blustery day, grey skies and chilly temperatures; the reeds move in the wind and waves, the surges of energy beginning near open water and rippling toward the land. Trees bend and leaves flutter to the forest floor. The waterfowl are moving south, and the young of the year join their parents in the ancient ritual of migration—geese, grebes, ducks, and loons. "Good weather, if you're a duck!"

Water, the waterfowl's element. Water as pure clean rain, replenishing the wetlands, restoring the basis of life to northern lakes. On the prairies, the puddle ducks' homes, broad and shallow, inch back up to their full capacity. In the deep, cold lakes of the boreal forest, the water filters through the conifers and pine duff to the loons' lakes.

Pristine waters, far from human development. Cold, clear waters, sky blue and reflective. These are loon waters, deceptively healthy looking. What we see isn't always accurate. Many of these lakes are clear because they are dead and acidic.

A hundred miles from civilization doesn't ensure protection from human impact. Along birds' migratory paths, an invisible trail of chemicals travels northward. Plumes disperse, molecules react and interact, and water changes to acid. Clouds concentrate these droplets and rain discharges the clouds. The acid droplets look and taste like water, but that's where the similarities end.

Loons live in an acid environment already—but that doesn't mean they can tolerate more acidity. In the boreal forests, the majority of rocks are volcanic in origin, and the soil is a glacially ground mixture of these bedrocks. As the rocks dissolve, the water that leaches through the soil acquires a slight acidity. As a result of these soil conditions, the plants in this zone also take on an acidity.

Ordinarily, when conifers lose their needles, the pine duff colors puddles and runoff with tannic acid. The brown waters defend the pines' territory against less adaptive plants that might otherwise crowd out the pine forest.

Rain droplets coat the needles and drip from branch to branch, brewing a tea as they go. The canopy reaches out, and the trunk concentrates the flow before it reaches the duff. Rain has always interacted with the forest floor, but the new levels of acidity in the rain now begin the brew much sooner and make it much stronger.

In addition to the plant and soil components that are natural to the forest, there is also a dusting of dry deposition—fine, dry, airborne particulates that are latent acidity. Like instant tea, they only await water to activate and become an acid solution.

Surface water either fulfills the needs of the plants, evaporates, or moves to ponds, lakes, or rivers. As the surface flow progresses, the water's acidity releases traces of heavy metals that are locked up in the soil. The liquid is then taken up by plants or continues toward the lakes and rivers, which accumulate both acidity and toxic metals.

The organisms that live in the lakes have nowhere else to go when their home is violated. They must respond to alteration or die. One-celled organisms die first, but when you damage any part of the food chain, the impact is felt throughout. Some organisms die directly from acidity, some see their offspring perish, others starve as their food sources diminish.

The lake becomes clearer and more beautiful. Without plankton the sunlight can penetrate to great depths. Without plants the lake bottom is uncluttered. Without life, the fisherman must move on.

For the loon, there are only so many lakes to use. Some are too developed by humans and nest sites are gone. On some the recreational activity is too great and nesting is impossible. On others the available nesting sites are already filled.

The loon, without the ability to understand, nests where history says a loon belongs. The young hatch and the struggle for survival begins.

The adults can move to other lakes for food, but the chick seldom does. The examples of chick movement that we give in Chapter 7 are good stories because they are exceptions. The adults forage for themselves on other lakes, but the young stay on their natal lake and try to survive on the stringy algae, which is the only remaining life that the parents can find.

Protein is lacking, the body building nutrients are missing. The chick can't climb on the adult's back. It eats mouthful after mouthful of algae. The stomach stays full while the chick starves. The adults abandon the dead offspring to seek better food for themselves. They will migrate on without producing a new loon. If one adult dies, there is no replacement. Next year they will return, if alive, to try again. They don't know that this story will be repeated year after year.

Gary Dulin, of the University of Minnesota, found that on lakes that were not dead from acid rain, the chicks could still be affected by the problem. If the lake was becoming acidified, food stocks were low enough that the loon chick was undernourished. It held on for a while, but often died of starvation in the second month. Robert Alvo, of Trent University, added that in Ontario, the loon chick's growth was slowed and the adult had to stay with it longer than normal, an additional stress on the parent.

The loons don't know we are studying the problem. They won't understand treaties, politics, and economics. They will just travel over a thousand miles, lay their eggs, work to raise a chick, and move on as they always have.

They will call as they fly and they will move in rain and clouds, while someone far below says, "Good weather for ducks."

LEAD AND MERCURY

Heavy metals, toxic metals, from sources obvious and sources obscure. "Two emaciated common loons (Gavia immer) were believed to have died of lead poisoning when fragments of fishing lines and lead sinkers were discovered in their stomachs." That's how Locke, Kerr, and Zoromski begin a report on lead poisoning.

In a conversation that I had with Sigurd Olson shortly before he passed away, the great conservationist and writer told me of his worries. He said that all the battles that had been fought for the canoe country were important, that if any of them had been a defeat, we would not have the canoe country anymore, but rather a shallow replica. But, he continued. those were easier battles than the ones that face us today. They were battles that had definite sides and tangible results. Today's battles are more difficult, because the culprits are on the other side of a weather system or drainage. The source is not one industry, but all industries, not one person, but all of us. The hidden dangers are the greatest test yet to preserving our wild heritage. As with all the battles before, if we lose this one, we lose everything.

We hear about the insidious nature of lead when hunters discuss the effect on waterfowl who ingest leftover lead shot while foraging on the pond bottom. The effect is emaciation and death. The very animals that are necessary for the survival of hunting as a sport are dying from leftover shot. Meanwhile the debate goes on about the effectiveness of the steel shot pattern and steel shot's effect on the hunter's gun. Rubbish! Without the game, there is no need for guns or shot patterns, and there is no hunter.

A loon was observed in 1976 on Squam Lake in New Hampshire. For two hours it floated, alive but not alert. After four hours, it was still floating—dead. There was no fat beneath the skin, the muscles had atrophied, and the feathers around the vent were stained with a green color from the feces. Inside the bird was a lead sinker and a dozen stones.

In 1980, at Little Lake, Wisconsin, a loon washed up on shore. It had died in an emaciated condition as well. The keel stuck out, the muscles were deteriorated, and the bird had no fat on its body. Inside was a lead sinker, fishing line, and rocks.

In many ways lead is a simple problem to deal with. We know that it comes from sinkers and shotgun pellets. We know how to correct the problem. The question is, will we?

The other problems are more insidious and harder to correct. In *Audubon* magazine in 1984, Frank Graham wrote an essay, "Mystery at Dog Island," about a true-life mystery. In January 1983, dead loons began to wash up on the shoreline of northern Florida at Dog Island, a barrier island that shelters Appalachicola Bay and St. George Sound. This is a good area for wintering loons, but in 1983 it was also a place for loons to die. By February, there were ten to twenty birds a day dying on the beaches. Observers saw the loons drag themselves up onto the dunes to die.

Death was due to starvation and anemia. The loons had empty guts and stomachs. Their pectoral muscles had atrophied and each bird's weight was two to three pounds, far under the normal range of six to eight pounds. In March, there were more than 250 dead birds. Why?

There were many possibilities. Lead poisoning could not account for an epidemic. Avian botulism, which has periodically decimated the populations in Lake Michigan because of their diet of alewives, didn't seem likely on the ocean. Investigators considered hemorrhagic enteritis, which causes anemia and weakens the bird until it cannot feed itself. There were concentrations of Microphallid trematodes (flukes) in the kidney, brain, and liver; the blue crab is an intermediate host, and loons have been known to eat crabs. No one knew, however, if the concentrations found were unusual. PCB and pesticides were ruled out. The mystery persisted.

A conservative estimate put the kill at 2500 along the Florida shore, 457 at Dog Island. There were also large kills along the Virginia and North Carolina shores, which made it too widespread an epidemic for the blue crabs to cause.

This spectacular die-off caused grave concerns and much speculation, but a study that ran from 1974 to 1984 showed that the common loon has heavy mortality throughout its migration and winter range. This study, by Malcolm Simons, Jr., took in all the dead birds along the coasts of the Gulf and the Atlantic. Observers were assigned areas of beach where they would walk and make observations. All the dead species were noted.

The cause of the loon deaths included shooting, entanglement in fish nets, monofilament fishing line, and the plastic collars that come on six-packs of canned beverages, and oil covering. The number of loons that were killed by oil covering was about 7 percent, just slightly higher than that of all other species, but not a large enough number to make the oil problem the major loon threat. Some of the oil that covered carcasses may even have come after death, when the bodies floated in to the shore. In the winter of 1983, 32 dead and 145 live birds were brought in from the sinking of the tanker *Marine Electric* off the coast of Virginia.

The study noted that the loon is susceptible to offshore bad weather and hurricanes. They are also influenced by the freshwater runoff and the effect it has on the saltwater prey species that loons depend on. In 1983, a series of winter storms created artificially large high tides, with the extra turbulence of wind-driven waters. During this period, the flounder, which is one of the loon's preferred foods, was difficult, if not impossible, to find and catch. This would affect the fishing strategy of the loon and change its behavior accordingly; it is one reason for the increased consumption of crabs and the flukes that were found.

There had been a larger than normal die-off in the winter of 1972-73 as well, and the studies from that period showed that oiling, hemorrhagic enteritis, and aspergillosis (a lung infection common in some northern hawks) were the main causes of the deaths. Aspergillosis can be induced by stress.

The mystery of Dog Island remains. In 1983, nearly 4000 birds were killed along the Atlantic and Gulf coast. In Simons's studies of dead birds along the same coastlines, the total of all species for 1975 to 1979 was equal to the number of loons that perished in this one winter.

In some loons there were high levels of mercury, twenty to thirty parts per million—lethal doses; in others there were just traces of mercury. Mercury can be released by industry discharge or can leach into the waters from the soil when acid rain percolates through. On some of the carcasses there were lesions that are associated with toxic metals. Was mercury the culprit? Was there a single episode to create this massive die-off, one that did not repeat itself in the next year? Did stress from all the environmental factors that were found in this difficult winter actually release the mercury from the normal fat reserves of the loon in such a way that the birds were poisoning themselves?

In 1986 Dan Helwig, a biologist for the Minnesota Department of Natural Resources, analyzed two years' collection of loon carcasses. His figures included some levels that were considered lethal, and some buildups that exceeded the lethal stage by dramatic amounts. The birds should have died before that level was reached.

Loon eggs in New Hampshire were analyzed for chemical content, and the good news was that the PCB, DDE, and DDT amounts had decreased appreciably. But while the alphabet soup diminished, the toxic metals, including mercury, did not.

Because it is naturally occurring as well as a pollutant, the impact of mercury is hard to analyze. The researchers do know that the loon and all other animals, including humans, can suffer from mercury poisoning. The symptoms are numbness, quivering limbs, blurred speech, impaired vision, and difficulty in walking. Not all of these would affect the loon, but enough of the symptoms could seriously impair its ability to survive.

The mystery has been analyzed, and do we have an answer? No! What we have uncovered is a list of symptoms, threats, and dangers that is longer than any of us would have ever expected. We know that more than 4,000 birds died on U.S. shores in one winter. We do not know how many impaired birds were eaten by sharks and other deep water predators, how many washed up on Mexico, how many died on migration. We also don't know how to prevent another mystery year. What we do know is that there are certain threats to all life, including our own, and we need to take action on all of them.

(P. Roberts)

HUMANS AND LOONS

ARTIFICIAL PLATFORMS

The common loon, Minnesota's state bird, usually nests on islands or on shorelines of northern lakes. On some lakes or reservoirs loons experience frequent nest failure because of water level fluctuations or because their mainland nesting sites are vulnerable to predation by raccoons or other predators.

"In such cases, a floating nesting platform can provide a more secure site for loons to nest on. Because of the high degree of development on many lakes in northeastern states like New Hampshire, such platforms now provide a substantial portion of the loon production in that area." (*Woodworking for Wildlife*, Minnesota Department of Natural Resources.)

The loon nesting platform has taken on the popularity of the wood duck box and eastern bluebird nest box in the loon states. The nest needs cedar posts, wire, staples, cement blocks, and natural vegetation, materials that are easy to get. The carpentry skills needed are minimal. The finished product looks natural, the loons take to it quickly, and the results are easy to observe and feel good about. It seems like such a tangible way to do something really good that it has become a civic and organizational project. Something that good must be right, it seems. But in some places there are better things to do, though those tasks are less rewarding. In other places the platform may even create a problem.

The artificial loon nests were pioneered by Judy McIntyre and John Mathisen in the Chippewa National Forest in 1970 after Mathisen discovered that loons were using artificial islands created for other waterfowl. On eleven lakes suitable for single loon pair territories, McIntyre was monitoring reproductive success. Six of the lakes had natural islands. The other five were supplied with island sites; on four of the lakes, sedge mat was sawed and supported by a frame of logs, and the other island was constructed like the one described in the Minnesota woodworking manual.

The islands were anchored with some protection in a sheltered bay or in emergent vegetation. The results were staggering. On the lakes without islands, there had been no successful reproduction; but with the platforms, the success was 67 percent, similar to the 60 percent success of the natural island lakes. The number of territorial pairs remained the same—there was no movement of loons from other sites as a result of the nest platforms. This factor was important, as reflected in this closing sentence in the paper that McIntyre and Mathisen published: "Artificial islands will probably not by themselves increase lake habitat for nesting loons because selection of lakes for breeding territories is determined by factors other than island availability."

New Hampshire took the experience of Chippewa National Forest and applied it on a wide scale to their lakes. The results were outstanding again. The birds of New Hampshire began to recover, and the crisis was averted for the time being. In Vermont the platforms were used to assist their effort, but in the first year, none of the four platforms was used.

Reports of many different observations began to come in from platform builders. Roy Tasche on Reno Lake in Minnesota was disappointed with the results from his platform.

The platform was located off a point in the lake, near an island where loons had nested in the past. The island had been inundated with high water, and the loons didn't have the same nesting environment now. That was the reason that Roy chose to put the nest out. The year before, there had been no chicks hatched on the lake. It was the only unsuccessful year in the seven years that the Tasches had watched the lake.

The loons nested on the platform the very first year that he put it out; three birds hatched, a success that is rare in any loon report. The first chick died within two days. Shortly after the hatch, the remaining loons, adults and two young, swam toward the point. There was a fisherman in a boat off the point, a neighbor who had fished there for years. The loons came toward the boat, while one of the young went into the reeds near the shore. The adults "raised hell" for a short time, then swam off, leaving the chick in the reeds. They did not return for it.

The young bird came up on land, and Pat Tasche found it. She put on gloves, carried it to the lake, and replaced it in the water. The adults did not return for it, and the chick died. Not long after this, the third loon chick also died. "It was almost like they were trying to ignore the chicks. I don't understand it at all."

Another platform builder in Minnesota, Dick Schabert, reported that he built his nest on April 27 and put it out into the lake with his nephew's help. Two loons were in the bay where the platform was being placed. "Look, uncle, they are waiting to use your platform." By the next weekend the nest was active. In three weeks, the eggs were cold and the nest abandoned.

Dick suspects that the high water level allowed fishermen and curious boaters access to the area where he had placed the nest site. The loons were probably bothered too much and left. In normal water levels the boats could not get to the site. The platform became a turtle loafing spot for the summer. Now the local sportsmen's club is planning to build ten new platforms.

The trouble is that it might not be a good idea for all these platforms to be placed in the lakes of Minnesota. Even with successful reports from Spooner, Wisconsin, and all over the Northeast, there are still important questions to be answered about the project.

In the Northeast, hydroelectric companies now expect to alleviate the environmental problems that are caused by draw-downs and other sudden changes in reservoir levels by placing floating platforms in the water. It is an easy way of diverting attention from the real problems.

In many states the platform has been a very important part of restoration. But in the states with strong loon populations, the goal is not to have the greatest number of loons possible but to have a population that can be sustained with minimum human impact. Each platform has a limited life, and if interest and observation do not continue, there will be a point at which the loon will suffer sudden nest-site loss. Indiscriminate use of artificial nest islands could create a bird population that is too dependent on human management.

The human species is management-oriented. We may say that it is our farming heritage, but we like to have our wildlife dependent on us. We like to manipulate. Those animals that most resist our efforts and are most independent tend to be the least liked. The loon is most appealing now in an age where we might give it assistance. The goal we should have is to allow the bird its maximum freedom, to keep the bird wild.

Nest platforms become showplaces if they are improperly used. People know the loons are there, and too often they want a peek. The increased activity can destroy the nest that people most want to succeed. So what is the answer, what is the balance?

Paul Strong of the Sigurd Olson Environmental Institute says that some of the following criteria must be met before a platform is put out: (1) There should be a problem with water level fluctuation that is causing nests to fail. (2) There should be recreation or predation problems due to the loons' choice of nest sites; the platform can be a way of inducing the loon to use an area of less conflict. (3) There should be loss of habitat; if the places that a loon has used in the past are destroyed by development, the platform might save a lake's loons.

Use of platforms has been mostly a loon lover's success story. But now it is time for the loon-loving public to take the next step in understanding the loon's ecology and make decisions that are best for the loon rather than for the people who love them.

OTHER HUMAN ACTIVITIES

Any alteration in the forest ecology disturbs the natural cycle of life in the common loon world, and humans have many subtle ways of creating change. In the normal course of wilderness life, the island is not subject to as much disturbance as the mainland. But human activities have increased in the loon lakes. Islands are often near good places to fish and, therefore, attract boats. The common loon is a beautiful bird and they attract attention to themselves. Most of all, the island is a good place for human campsites and an ideal setting for recreation of many kinds.

Boat waves can sweep over the nest and roll the eggs out. Human activity can drive the loons off the nest and keep them away from their eggs while gulls, ravens, and crows take advantage of the adults' absence. Researchers have found that island campsites in northern Minnesota and summer boating and cabins in Finland have affected the success of both the common and the Arctic loon's island nests. On Big Muskelunge Lake in Wisconsin, a loon observer in 1986 reported that for thirty-eight years there had been at least two chicks from two pair of nesting loons on the lake. A May 1986 fishing contest on the lake attracted a lot of boats, and the result was no loon reproduction for the year.

Researcher Jim Caron, who studied the impact of motor versus nonmotor activities, found that recreationists caused one common loon pair to nest four different times. The stress and the physical demands on the bird to lay eggs four times is beyond description.

It is difficult to look at the impact of our activities and judge them ecologically. While we look at the activity of motorboats and their impact on the loon, we must also realize that a single motorboat passing at a moderate speed, with a minimal wake, actually may produce less stress for the loons than a canoe because of the time that it takes for the canoe to get through the loon's territory.

Pacific loons suffer some human predation from Inuit who remove loon eggs for food, but most of their

human-related problems result from the collection of food near the nest, rather than the removal of the eggs. The closeness of the human drives the loons off the nest and makes the eggs vulnerable to attack from gulls and jaegers, who do not hestitate to take the eggs even while the humans are present.

Sometimes, the detrimental impacts of our actions are harder to observe. Denny Olson, of the Minnesota Loon Preservation Project, discussed the conflict of fish management and loon nesting. It isn't the old story of loon-and-fisherman competition but rather one of lake alteration. Lake rehabilitation is often a process of intentional lake kill-off, during which a poison is used to remove nearly all the existing fish population, and then restocking, which puts in the fishing enthusiasts' preferred fish.

In lakes where the loon nests, this might mean the elimination of their preferred food species. The impact could be as devastating as acid rain sterilization. When the loon returns to nest, it does not know of management decisions. From the surface, it cannot know of changes beneath. A nest without a food source is a nest that is destined to fail.

Another fishing-related acitivity that affects loons is leech collection for bait sales. In the Mississippi headwaters, leech collection has been done near a loon nest site during incubation, keeping the adult off the nest at a critical time.

In ecology, every action has a chain of reactions, and it is our duty to understand the entire chain.

LOON REHABILITATION

Many problems can arise as loons travel from ocean to lake and back. There are complications of disease and infirmity in a loon's life just as there are in a human's, but there are also complications caused by the human alteration of the continent. Sometimes those complications are eased by humans who take more than a passing interest in the animals.

In August 1982, a juvenile common loon was observed by a resident on Upper Gull Lake in Minnesota. To those who watched the bird in the lake, it appeared that a fishing line and bobber were entangled around one of its feet. The bird was doomed unless someone could help it. Its swimming ability was impaired and it was obviously underweight, judging by the way its keel protruded. DNR personnel came out to the lake and captured the bird.

When the loon was examined, the "bobber" turned out to be a large round growth attached to its middle toe. The growth, a tumor, was sent away for analysis, and the bird was banded and released. Without the impediment, it moved naturally and showed no disability.

A new branch of wildlife action has proliferated in the 1980s. It's called wildlife rehabilitation, and there are centers throughout the U.S. and Canada, often specializing in the rehabilitation of specific types of wildlife, such as raptors or song birds.

Almost all nature-oriented programs have some de-gree of involvement in rehabilitation. If it is a simple problem, the individuals in the program might try to resolve it. If it is more complex, they try to get the animal to the proper group. At Northwoods Audubon Center, near Sandstone, Minnesota, a loon was brought to the naturalists by a game warden. It had not escaped to the south with other migrants. The warden had removed it from a pond and brought it to the Center to see if anything was wrong with it.

One problem in animal rehabilitation is that the patient cannot respond to questions. The warden could guess that the pond the loon had landed on was too small to take off from, but who could be sure? It could have a toxic poisoning, it could have wing damage that would prevent long flights, or it could be suffering malnutrition. The people giving care can only be patient and persistent.

The bird was checked over and nothing was found that would prohibit the bird's survival, but precaution is always part of any bird's treatment. The loon was given the exclusive use of a bathtub and a supply of minnows from the bait store. The bird was fine, and five days later, when it was released in Grindstone Lake, it took its freedom greedily. Who knows if the bird could have survived on its own had the warden not brought it in?

One of the most common forms of assistance in the North has been the removal of birds who have been trapped by ice on the lake and their own poor judgment. Because it is late in the year, the trapped birds are probably juveniles, since the adults leave first. It is even more likely to be a bird that hatched from a second, later nest. Because of the late hatching, the bird's flight development would also be late.

On a bird's migration, ponds with a very thin veneer of ice would seem like very calm water until the bird landed. Then when it tried to regain the air, it would not be able to propel itself over the ice.

In the early years of the Sigurd Olson Environmental Institute's Project Loon Watch, two of the staff members took a boat and axe and chopped their way out to a stranded loon near Hayward. They then took the bird to Chequamegon Bay of Lake Superior and released it so that it could try its route south again.

★   ★   ★

In Minocqua, Wisconsin, the Northwoods Wildlife Center averages three to four birds per year trapped in the ice. They are usually swimming around in a small patch of open water when the crew arrives with rowboat and net. The bird is confused, the crew is intent, the lake is cold, and the project becomes an annual comedy with potential serious consequences. The boat is pushed out onto the ice until the ice gives way and the boat breaks through. Then everyone jumps in and breaks their way through the remaining ice until they reach the loon. The loon's reaction is to dive. The boaters sit poised with nets to try and nab the bird as it resurfaces.

The Center's director, Bill Bauer, talks about the call he got in 1985 reporting a stranded loon on a pond that was too small for takeoff. Bill kept putting the rescue off, hoping to let nature take its course. Then one day, a frantic call came in describing a wounded loon flopping around in the woods. Bill came out, picked up the loon, which was 200 yards from Minocqua Lake by this time, found that the bird was fine, placed it in the lake, and watched it take off.

Another stranded-loon situation arose during a spring migration in the '80s when an early snowstorm disoriented a flock of loons. The birds caught in this weather system looked for a place to land and find shelter. In the limited visibility, they spotted a river beneath them and landed. The river was made of blacktop. The Center personnel found ten to fifteen birds scattered over 100 yards of Highway 51, flopping around in a very unfamiliar landscape. The birds were picked up and transported to open water, where they were released unharmed.

On another occasion, a fertile loon egg was brought to the Center and placed in an incubator, where it hatched successfully. Center personnel raised the chick for several days and then took it to a lake where there was a loon pair with only one chick. The hatchling was released from a boat and swam toward the other loons. Halfway to the loons it changed its mind, turned, and swam back to the boat. The rehabilitators gently tossed the chick back in the water so that it was closer to the adult loons. This time it kept going, and the humans returned to shore hoping that the chick would succeed.

The Wildlife Center has a much more serious rehab job to do, and the loons get involved in that too. Founded in 1979, the Center is part of a veterinary clinic and has access to the vets and their facilities. All types of animal are brought in and undergo a variety of treatments, from rest and medication to X ray and surgery. The most common loon injury is from fish hooks.

If the hook is in the stomach, the bird must be left alone; a vet cannot open the stomach without causing more damage to the bird than the hook does. It is hoped that the hook will dissolve in the stomach acids.

Most of the hook cases are operable. In one case, the bird had a lure with two hooks in its throat. The surgeons made a small incision to allow one barb to penetrate the throat cavity, so that they could cut it off. They then made a second incision and took the remaining barb and the entire lure out. The loon was placed in their recovery pond and was released within a week.

★   ★   ★

Susan Davis of Delta Lodge, Iron River, Wisconsin, had an injured loon brought to her that had been found walking on a road with a treble hook caught in the wrist of the right wing. Its feet were bleeding from its walk, and the bird was distraught from the entire experience. She put a shirt over the bird to calm it, a tactic that is good for all wildlife; animals seem less threatened if they cannot see the actions around them. Then she slowly worked the hooks through, so that she could cut off the barbs with a pliers and wire cutter. After the hook was removed, the loon was taken to the lake, where it swam fifty feet toward another loon, then rose and displayed, to the applauding accompaniment of the resorters.

Paul Strong tells of an older couple in Maine who take in a variety of injured animals. An adult loon was brought in for care. It was a migrant that had made a road stop. They discovered that the loon didn't really require a bathtub, but could get by with a tray of water where it could stand and dip its bill to preen. They put out a rolled-up wet towel, and the loon would waddle up to it as best it could and place its chest on the roll. This offset the pressure on the loon's chest that resulted from not being in weight-displacing water. They put petroleum jelly on the loon's legs to keep them from cracking.

The bird seemed to be getting along fine, so the couple took what they considered a grateful bird to the ocean for releasing. It was nervous and disoriented; they had to protect their eyes because the bird instinctively pecked at them. They reached the shoreline and then walked the bird out into the surf so that it could swim away. The couple stood knee-deep in the rolling surf, anxiously watching their patient seek freedom. The loon swam off, then stopped and swam back toward them. "Look, he doesn't want to leave us." Touched by the bird's devotion, the man reached back into the water to greet the returning bird. The loon snapped at his hand with its bill, drew blood, and swam away.

One last rehabilitation story also comes from the Northeast. A loon was washed up on a storm-ravaged road in Nova Scotia and brought home by the woman who found it. The warden was called and he advised her to put it in the bathtub for a few days and feed it. If it did all right, it could be released. The entire family became very attached to the loon. They fed it fish and listened to it yodel in response to a cassette of loon calls. One day, the young boy in the family came into the bathroom naked and walked over to the tub. The loon lashed out and snapped at his penis.

We tend to think that animals have the same thoughts that we do, one reason why so many people try to raise wild animals as pets and fail. We feed raccoons on back porches and then watch the loons on the lake, never thinking that the raccoons are extending their ranges because of human activities and attacking loon eggs as they move north. Wildlife owes us no thanks; they only want to survive.

Through large underwater viewing windows, zoo visitors can watch the loon swim and dive. The bird's streamlined shape allows it to manuever easily underwater. (T. Cajacob, Minnesota Zoo)

ZOO LOON

Two beavers were cutting down a pair of aspen saplings while a group of green-winged teal noiselessly swam near the pond edge. I was inches away from a young loon, looking at its submerged breast and one of its webbed feet. Anyone who has any experience around loons realizes it's absolutely impossible to sneak up on the bird in its aquatic environment, but I had no special potion to make me invisible to the loon. It was alive, healthy, and aware of my presence. In fact, when I looked at it above water, it calmly blinked its right eye and returned to its midday nap.

This was no dream, no delusion of a mosquito-crazed canoeist. In fact, I was hundreds of miles from the Boundary Waters. There is only one place in this country, in the whole world, where such an encounter could occur—the Minnesota Zoo's beaver exhibit.

The loon I was watching through the glass viewing window is a very special bird. Definitely one of a kind. Never before has a loon been raised from an incubated egg, kept in captivity, survived, and prospered for such a long time. In the past, the only loons ever put on display were "rehab" birds, that is, birds that had been found in the wild with some injury or problem that made them unable to fly or feed themselves. They were sick wild birds under the stress of capture, who were then transferred to situations that create even more stress—small bodies of water, other animals to share their territory, and people everywhere.

The Minnesota Zoo had one such unsuccessful experience with an adult loon. Curators Jimmy Pichner and Mike DonCarlos both had a desire to exhibit the state bird, but they knew it could never be successful unless a new approach was tried—the collection of eggs from the wild, incubation, hatching, and hand rearing of chicks. They believed that a carefully thought-out loon exhibition project could become reality.

On May 29, 1985, with the assistance of the Minnesota DNR Nongame Division, three eggs were collected from two nests. The adult loons that provided the eggs renested and were seen with chicks three months later.

Within eight hours of removal from their nest, the eggs were placed in zoo incubators. They were weighed in, and an approximate stage of incubation was determined based on field data of weight and sizes of eggs. The incubator was similar to the standard chicken-farm variety, but it had been modified to accommodate the larger loon eggs and the different temperature and humidity requirements. The eggs were incubated at 99.5° F.

The anxious waiting began. As if in a very long labor, the two concerned curators spent the next two weeks checking on their precious charges and feeling somewhat helpless about the outcome. It did no good to "candle" the eggs, because the shells are opaque. Three times a week the eggs were weighed to plot weight loss, which occurs as water is lost through the shell by osmosis. Eggs lose approximately 15% of their original weight through this process.

The eggs were turned every hour until four days before expected hatch, when they were moved to the hatcher and no longer turned. In the wild, there comes a time during incubation when the adult loons stop rotating the eggs in the nest. This allows the chick to orient itself inside the egg, so that when it is ready to hatch it is positioned in the proper end of the egg, where there is an air pocket. If it were to go to the wrong end, it would drown in its own amniotic fluids before emerging.

On June 7, 1985, the first chick broke free of its oval brownish-green shell. It hatched without assistance. Five days later, the second chick, unrelated to the first, emerged, and this time Jimmy was there with his camera to record the happy event. The third egg never hatched, even though it was left in the incubator for an extra period of time, in hopes that their calculations had been wrong. Unfortunately, they weren't. It was determined that the egg had been dead when collected.

75

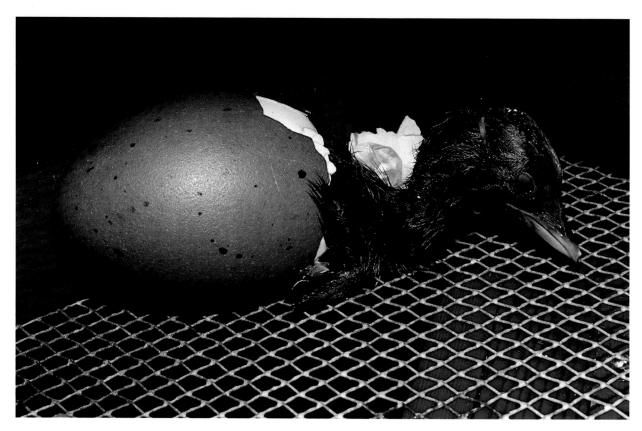

June 12, 1985. The second loon chick hatches at the Minnesota Zoo. (J. Pichner)

Nine days old. The loon chick occasionally became somewhat waterlogged and had to be removed from the holding pool until it preened itself back into shape. (J. Pichner)

Fifteen days old and feeling frisky. (J. Pichner)

The first chick to hatch weighed 98 grams; the second, the ultimate survivor, weighed 86.5 grams. They were about the size of a pair of baseballs, but weighing much less.

When their matted, soaking feathers had dried and turned them into balls of black fluff, the chicks were transferred to a waterfowl brooder for hand rearing. The brooder is a wooden box, 48 inches long and 30 inches wide, with a pool of water that leads gradually down to a depth of one foot.

As soon as the chicks were moved to the brooder and introduced to the water, they plunged in, immediately displaying loon behavior. They made the soft hoot sound, which Jimmy describes as a "bad chirp." They preened themselves, spreading the oil from the base of their tails over their downy bodies. These feathers are somewhat water resistant on their own, and they trap so much air that when the chicks tried to dive they immediately popped back up on the surface. In perfect imitation of adults, they rose and madly flapped their miniature versions of wings. They swam and put their faces in the water, peering at imaginary fish. All this behavior was performed without their ever seeing an adult of their species. When they tired of the water, they would waddle and push their way back onto the dry portion of the brooder.

Now the job of filling in for the parent loons became much more time consuming. For the first week, the chicks had to be fed every hour, sixteen hours a day. Food consisted of flathead minnows, first chopped and later whole. Some live minnows were presented to the chicks, and they instinctively killed them and occasionally ate a few. Mealworms were added for variety, and grit was continuously provided. During the second week, feedings dropped to every two hours, gradually decreasing to four per day, between 6:30 A.M. and 10:30 P.M. In the third week, trouble developed. One of the chicks, the first to hatch, stopped eating. Jimmy and Mike stayed with it late into the night, tending it, but to no avail. It died at eighteen days of age of a bronchial infection.

There was just the one remaining chick to pin all their hopes and efforts on. It continued to feed and thrive, and at five weeks of age it was in the water full-time. Its food now consisted of smelt and capelin, along with a daily dose of vitamins. In feeding the young chick, the curators discovered that it showed more interest in the food if it was fed fish of different sizes, with or without heads, minced or filleted.

The next period of concern for the curators occurred when the chick began the molt to juvenile plumage at about ten weeks of age. Water quality was constantly monitored, and after each feeding the surface water was skimmed to clear it of any floating debris. The bird's feathers were very easily fouled by surface material, including its own fecal matter. Even with this precaution, the loon was very susceptible to waterlogging; the curators spent many hours, working day and night, to make sure it was all right.

Eventually the loon finished its molt and was ready to move to the beaver exhibit on September 3, 1985. The family of beavers paid little attention to the loon, but it carefully avoided them. The initial introduction period took two weeks; it was that long before the loon was completely comfortable with its new home and able to be left on exhibit. There were several occasions when the bird became agitated, dove until it became waterlogged, and had to be retrieved and returned to its original holding pool. There it settled down and preened its feathers back into shape.

While in the holding pool, the chick had seen ducks and had acted aggressively toward them. When the loon finally relaxed enough to remain on exhibit, three wood ducks and two shovelers were introduced to the pond. Seeing these waterfowl, the loon immediately reared up and tremoloed three times. It had never made this sound before. But the aggressive reaction was short-lived; after a couple minutes the loon lost interest in the ducks, and it has paid little attention to them since. Jimmy Pichner thinks this is not extraordinary. It is a young bird and has no reason to defend its territory.

There was yet another emergency to face. On November 12, 1985, the waterfowl were removed from the exhibit because they had gotten into the habit of scattering the loon's food. The loon itself was behaving somewhat erratically and was eating less. Its weight began to drop, and it was removed from the exhibit to the original holding pool. A medical examination showed no detectable problems. The loon did well in the holding pool and began to eat, but after five days it again stopped eating. The bird lost 22 percent of its weight, and the curators decided it was necessary to force-feed it two to three times a day. For each of the next twenty-six days, they fed the loon 295 to 470 grams of fish. Finally the loon began to eat on its own. No reason for the lack of appetite was ever found.

On May 7, 1986, the loon was put on exhibit once again. This time the bird had no problems adjusting, and it spent the summer swimming and diving in the beaver pond. It showed little fear of the people who stared at it through the viewing windows. It responded to the keepers that fed it and to its foster fathers, Mike and Jimmy.

In November 1986, when the temperatures began to drop, the loon once again stopped eating. It was immediately removed from the exhibit and placed in the indoor holding pool, and its appetite returned. It remained in holding during the winter months, the molting process began, and gradually the loon began to assume the appearance of an adult. The bill turned black, the eye began to turn red, and the grey body feathers were replaced by black and white spotted ones. The molt into adult plumage occurred right on schedule, based on the study of loons in the wild.

The loon is doing well and is expected to be back in the beaver exhibit in early spring, but there are still many questions to be answered. Is it the urge to migrate that has caused the eating problems in late fall? Will there be an extreme change in its behavior with the physical changes that have occurred? Will it become aggressive and, as Jimmy says, "hammer on the beaver, hammer on the ducks"? They don't even know if it's a male or female. If it eventually yodels, they'll know it's a male—but if it doesn't, that won't automatically mean it's a female. It is possible to surgically sex loons, but that's an approach they'd rather not use.

The loon will remain at the zoo, on exhibit in the beaver pond. The likelihood of pairing it up with another loon is slim because of the potential for aggression by a pair of breeding adults in the beaver exhibit. There is also the problem of providing a mate. It would have to be raised from a chick, because the poor survival rate for wild-caught loons is already known.

For all the stress of the first year and a half, Jimmy and Mike are pleased with their loon. They accomplished their goal of putting the state bird of Minnesota on exhibit, and they have been able to document the husbandry that is needed to keep a bird as sensitive as the loon in captivity.

We hope that there will always be loons in the wild for us to love and marvel at. But as the wilderness shrinks and humanity expands, there will be people who will never visit a northern lake to see and hear the magnificent *Gavia immer*. At the Minnesota Zoo, these people may be able to visit a beaver pond and see for themselves a living loon.

At thirty-one days, the chick's black down has been replaced by the brown juvenile plumage. (J. Pichner)

Looney came to the dock three or four times a day to be fed by Rita.(K. Crowley)

THE LOON LADY OF TEN MILE LAKE

Rita Herreid and her friend and neighbor, Elaine, had just returned from town and found twenty to thirty ducks out by their dock.

"Look at that loon over there!"

"A loon does not come up on the lawn, Elaine."

"Rita, that is a loon!"

"Elaine!" Then as she looked, it began to register. "It *is* a loon!"

They got their cameras and stayed up on the lawn to take a picture of the bird; they didn't want to scare it away. But with each step and each new picture, it became obvious that something was wrong.

Other neighbors had seen the bird by now and came over to get a closer look. Rita called the resort across the bay and found that the bird had been there as well. It was time for some action. They put a fish net over the bird. One neighbor picked it up, and they untangled a mass of monofilament fishing line that had ensnarled the loon's legs. The line had actually cut into its legs, to the point that the bird would not be able to use them and survive on its own. When the loon was set on the ground, it did not move.

Strips of freshly caught fish were offered, and it responded to the food immediately. The loon wasn't kept in a pen, but it seemed to sense the safety of a small cove that was created to harbor the Herreids' small fishing boat. Rita got more fish and continued to feed it.

She called the DNR and other organizations for help. What she got was lots of promises, but little action. No one really knew what to do with the loon, and no one wanted to be responsible for it. The survival rate of captive loons is exceedingly low, and most professionals didn't want to buck the odds. As it turned out, it was for the best that no one else got involved, because the loon, named Looney, took to Rita's care. She became the bird's personal protector.

In the beginning, Rita had to beg for help, but the loon that arrived on August 2, 1986, became a celebrity, and offerings of fish came in unsolicited. Now they were in the media and in the area's consciousness; Looney became a special project for all of Ten Mile Lake.

Three to four times a day, every day, Looney would come to Rita's dock to feed. If Rita walked out to the dock, the loon would acknowledge with its head, raising the bill slightly, turning a little to each side, and then dipping it into the water in a peering posture. The loon came right up to the dock and took food directly from Rita's hand, but it would not allow itself to be touched. It took the fish in its bill, "tenderized" it with a chewing action, and then swallowed the fish, which ranged from minnows to fairly sizable suckers.

For a while, the loon crawled up on land for its feeding, but it soon found the water a better environment for eating. It would take food until it was full and then swim back out into the lake to digest its meal.

Some mornings, Rita had to sneak through her house to have her morning coffee in peace. The loon would wait out in the lagoon, looking through the cabin's big picture windows. As soon as it saw Rita, it raised its head and swam over toward the cabin to begin a pleading pattern that was too much for Rita to ignore.

Both the loon's legs showed almost no movement at first. The left leg, which was stronger, could make light surface strokes and gave the loon the ability to swim and move. Rita watched both legs, waiting and hoping that healing would take place, allowing the bird to recover for migration. By the end of August, the loon had some use of the right leg, giving Rita new hope. During one feeding period, the loon actually dove and came up with its own fish. No moment could have been any sweeter for Rita, whose real desire was to see the bird able to leave on its own, rather than to find it "a good home" where it would exist in captivity.

Near the end of August, the bird began to rise, spread its wings, and display. As autumn approached, the bird's improvement sped up. It was a matter of pride not only for the Herreids, but also for the entire area. As people visited and fed the bird, they became more involved and caring. They might bring food for Looney, or they might take off after a boat that had been harassing other loons on the lake, to tell the offenders that loons are special birds and they didn't want them injured, disturbed, or frightened. Communication, Rita says, is all that is really needed to get people to care.

In September, Rita returned from a vacation, during which a neighbor had taken care of Looney. Looney was no longer hanging around in the small lagoon. A nesting pair that had earlier guarded its territory no longer did so, and Looney had chosen to roam the lake.

A film crew went out on the lake with Rita on a pontoon boat. Looney came close one time, then departed, making that long glorious loon run across the surface and then rising into the air. "Looney" was free once more.

The Herreids have spent summers on Ten Mile Lake for seventeen years. They have seen the loons that nest each year in their bay, as well as the loons of other bays. They have seen the rafts of migrants in August and they have listened to the calls that echo in the night. But now things are different, and they will never be the same again. They have had contact with a loon. That contact bridged the gulf that separates our species and put everyone who was involved on a much closer plane of existence. This type of interaction creates a consciousness that is closer to the Indian heritage, one in which we share the earth with all other wildlife.

One lesson that comes from Rita's experience is that an injured bird has a better chance if care can be given in its natural surroundings. A second lesson is that there is a chance that loons can adapt to human presence if we are aware of the limitations that we need to put on our own behavior. In fact, many loons are existing in areas of high human development, places where loons had disappeared for awhile. This could be a good indication of loon adaptation.

Author Mike Link had a chance to feed Looney one afternoon near the end of its recovery period. (K. Crowley)

After being fed, Looney swam and preened in the sheltered cove near the Herreids' cabin. (M. Link)

LOONESSAY

Just when I thought that the loon had been covered, that we knew all that we needed to know and there was nothing more to research, I was told by my knowledgeable observers that loon fever is running rampant in the Great Lakes region.

People complain of hot-pan holders with loons, cold-drink holders with loons, glasses, pictures, calendars, and appointment books all decorated with loons. They find them piled under Christmas trees, hiding in birthday wrappings, and even given as wedding presents. The teddy bear is no longer in style in the Midwest. People there give their children stuffed loons and decorate the kids' rooms with loon wallpaper.

I ignored this report at first, but when my wife wore a loon nightgown on our honeymoon, I thought I had better check things out.

This is what I found.

★   ★   ★

Alfred Hitchcock's *The Birds* was a terrifying look at the avian world, should they become an enemy bent on revenge for all those Thanksgiving dinners and Kentucky Colonels. It was a plot that shook us up because it seemed to point out humans' lack of superiority in the natural world. It was a mad fantasy.

But what about subtlety? What if birds could develop a scheme to infiltrate our lives, ad campaigns that made them symbolic of all that we see as virtue? Could their status change? Could they beat us at our own game? Ah, foolishness, loonacy.

Here I am in the state of Minnesota, bastion of German bullheadedness and Scandinavian skepticism. So what if they chose the loon as their state bird? Every state has an official bird, and the robin, meadowlark, cardinal, and bluebirds have been thoroughly booked up.

The loon was available, unique to the northern clear cold lakes, and even featured a scandinAVIAN yodel for a song—a fact that may explain why loons, in a record of loon song called *Voices of a Loon*, have now replaced Whoopee John and Prince as Minnesota's top-selling recording artists.

I left a little shop called Hello Minnesota, a nice little souvenir shop that features native crafts. I wore my loon T-shirt with my new tie that has little loons swimming all over the maroon background.

I bought a loon cup, a loon wind sock, a loon pennant, and I even got a loon pen that I used to scribble the rough draft of this essay onto my loon note pad. I'll probably use one of my loon stickers to seal the envelope that I send to my publisher.

Now that I had a roll of loon stickers, I agonized over ways to use them. I put some on my car, and put one on my forehead, thinking it would make me a local standout. But there was some woman on Hennepin Avenue walking around in a full-sized loon suit. Can you imagine a person walking down the street dressed like a loon?

Well, I still had my stickers and I started thinking about football helmets. Not that I have one to put my loons on, but football players put stars on their helmets for good tackles, touchdowns, and other achievements. Maybe I could get scuba divers to put loons on their masks each time they come up with some artifact from the bottom of the lake, or bird-watchers could put them on their binoculars every time they make a good sighting.

If nothing else I'll fill in the void on my refrigerator—those blank spaces between all the loon magnets.

Not all of the loon items are silly. I mean, what young lady wouldn't want to wear a loon garter to the prom? Who wouldn't want a carving of a little loon sitting on a big loon? I suspect that it is supposed to represent a chick on an adult, but someone forgot to tell this "artist" that the chick does not have adult markings. Fortunately for the manufacturers, their marketing ability exceeds their ornithology, because I saw this combination all over.

Loons, loons, loons! It seems like they are everywhere. I fill out my Minnesota tax form and there is a loon on it. It's in the slot for contributing to non-game wildlife programs. It's referred to as the chickadee checkoff, but I recognize a loon when I see one.

I know its not just Minnesota that is loon crazy. In Mercer, Wisconsin, they have an entire weekend called Loon Days. The loon album was recorded in New Hampshire.

There are Loon Rangers in Vermont, Maine, and Massachusetts. The Sigurd Olson Environmental Institute in Ashland, Wisconsin, coordinates a Project Loon Watch in both Wisconsin and Minnesota. This isn't a system to watch out for loons, a modern civil defense system, but more of a communal parenting, with lots of little binocular-holders observing, recording, and reacting to each loon's arrival, departure, and yodel.

If it is part of the loons' plan to take over, they show a remarkable understanding of U.S. aid programs. Having been attacked by armies of commercial fishermen in the past, having suffered from chemical warfare of DDT, PCB, and mercury, the loons qualify for aid, sympathy, and guilty consciences. Now it is fashionable to openly display love and concern (although there remain a few terrorists among our species).

Of course, in any attempt to subvert a country, you must control the press and the education system to take charge of the minds. Wait a minute—is that a loon symbol on top of the Duluth newspaper? Well, that's better than another foreign newspaper takeover.

In the schools, the Minnesota DNR has a Loons On Loan kit that goes out free to any school that will pick it up. It's filled with slides, cassettes, films, a stuffed loon, and a disassembled bird that serves as a basic hands-on trivia game.

There is also a subversive "Gavin Immer," a character who not only dresses like a loon but believes he is one. They let him in the schools, too, and even invite him to club meetings, programs for otherwise sensible adults.

Enough already. A lady walked by with loon earrings, and a shop had a loonoo clock instead of a cuckoo. I needed to sit down. The divers had gotten to me, too. "I give up." I went around the corner to get something to eat, and there, in neon, was "The Loon Cafe."

I thought that would settle things; I would eat a loon. But did they serve loons? Of course not. I tried to order one, but the waitress turned green and ran away. I'll just wait until she returns on her little webbed feet. Hold on! *Webbed feet?*

THE PHOTOGRAPHER'S STORY

Good nature photographers are good observers. They spend hours cooped up in a blind, they sit quietly through the cold hour before dawn, they sit patiently while clouds toy with the lighting, and they wait while the loon moves in and out of shadows. For a photographer like Peter Roberts, there is a code of ethics that makes the bird's peace more important than the photographer's pictures. Some of the classic loon shots are not in his repertoire because they are stress behaviors that are induced by the photographer and may harm the bird, its eggs, or its young.

Peter would get up early in the morning, dress, and cross the lake in his boat before the rays of the sun began to appear on the eastern horizon. He wanted to capture the special social behavior of the birds that begins about fifteen minutes before sunrise and ends about fifteen minutes after. This was not something that the procrastinator or the late sleeper could do. It took effort, but his reward was more than pictures.

On calm mornings, when the lake was without a ripple and the early colors of the sunrise spread across the water in broad washes, five to seven loons gathered in the narrows and held their morning celebration. They would run across the lake, without taking off from the surface. Sometimes they would become brazen and swim right up to Peter's boat.

Once he was watching six birds together, and as he approached, three dove. The remaining three put their heads under water and watched the submerged loons dance beneath the surface. From his boat, Peter could see the currents and turmoil in the surface water created by their submerged gymnastics.

On another morning, the birds formed a circle, and with wings outstretched so that they nearly touched one another, they rose out of the water and held themselves in place, with wings beating and feet paddling. They balanced themselves with necks and beaks pointing toward one another. This continued for fifteen to twenty minutes before one bird initiated a retreat and took off. Within a few seconds, each bird left, all of them taking off into the breeze.

These morning celebrants were particular in their ritual. It was held only when it was calm and the sun shone through a clear sky. As they left, they would glide, call, and circle—part of the sunrise—humpbacked silhouettes with a tremolo flight song.

Persistence in the photo blind often pays special dividends. Peter had the opportunity to observe and film an interaction between two loons and a beaver. The loons' original nest was washed out by high water, and the birds chose as a second site a location in a beaver's territory. The two species had never shared their home area, and it led to an interesting social exchange.

The beaver is a very territorial animal, just like the nesting loon, and it does not tolerate animals of any species within its territory, especially if they intend to establish squatter's rights. Beavers patrol their territory daily, sweeping around their pond, checking the dam site, observing the shoreline, taking stock of their forest inventory, and looking over their lodge. When the loons chose to nest in the territory, the beaver did not agree to relinquish that shore area as part of its regular patrol—and that caused a confrontation.

During three aggressive exchanges, the beaver swam toward the loon to drive it away. The beaver actually lunged toward the loon, attempting to make contact; the loon in return dove after the beaver. The beaver dove, and the loon took a run across the surface, each sparring with the other as though testing the right sequence of attack. The beaver surfaced, slapped its tail to one side and then to the other side in protest. After this sharp sound, it charged the loon again. The loon replied with its own call and flapped its wings in another surface run, with the beaver in pursuit. The exchange ended with the beaver swimming away.

In the foray, the loon lost a quarter inch of its upper mandible. It affected the loon for a few days; a broken bill is a big handicap for a fishing bird.

86

On another occasion, an otter came into the loons' territory, and the male responded with more wing flapping and calling to distract the otter. Within three minutes, another three adult loons appeared on the scene and joined the first in distracting calls, flaps, and runs. Meanwhile, the loon chick disappeared in the raucous chaos of dive, run, flap, call, and fly. It was a powerful example of communications and mutual defense.

The loon is big and conspicuous. Photographs capture only a small part of the overall wonder of the bird, and that is what makes it so special to be a loon observer. There are still fascinating things to be learned. Each of us can accumulate personal experiences and knowledge, even if the photographs we take are only those that are put on the indelible surface of the mind's memory.

PERSPECTIVES

Yes, we love the loon. In fact, right now, we're plain "in love" with loons. We love their beautiful, intricate pattern of black and white feathers; we love their repertoire of haunting songs; we love the way they perform for us — their water ballet; and we absolutely adore their fluffy, coal-black babies that look so cute riding on the parents' backs.

But do we love the loon enough to save it for the future? Or is this just a passing fad that makes Madison Avenue love the loon too? Do we love the loon enough to make sacrifices, financially and culturally? For that is what it will take to allow this bird to survive. We know acid rain is killing the lakes that loons absolutely depend on for the successful rearing of young. We know increased development of property around northern lakes means increased disturbance of nesting pairs — not only from human activity but from scavengers, like the raccoon and gull, that follow our footsteps. It is frighteningly tempting, even for the most environmentally conscious person, to get too close to these high-strung birds and their nests.

We're dealing with a bird population that even in good years is barely replacing its own numbers. For the first half of this century, the loon didn't even reach ZPG — they were on the negative side of the scale.

The loon desperately needs our help. All the hoopla and hype we're experiencing now is wonderful if it makes more people know and care about the loon. But they must be willing to do more than hang images of the bird on the wall.

In the long run, it is not just the loon we're saving, but a part of the world we cannot duplicate, imitate, or manufacture. How will we explain to our grandchildren how it feels to hear the distant wail that echoes from shore to shore? Will we play a record and try to describe for them how a loon looks at dusk, or will we take them to the lake and let them learn for themselves?

LOON ORGANIZATIONS

Organizations proliferate so in the United States that it is almost impossible to know all of them, let alone know how they came about. Some clubs stand the test of time and others seem much more temporary. Large national organizations tend to be focused on such a broad spectrum of issues that they only serve to keep the membership informed, like a national news service. They cannot focus on individual issues unless they are formed with a specific purpose, like the North American Loon Fund, which serves as a clearinghouse for all the local organizations. Which club you join may depend on where you live, grew up, or vacation.

An important fact about clubs is that the size is not as important as the dedication. In the state of Washington, a 1985 study showed that there were only two successful loon pairs in the entire state. This did not deter a club called the Loon Lake Loon Association. This association began with a group of women who took regular walking excursions together and had an annual loon walk at Loon Lake. They began to think about the lake name and the tales of old-timers who remembered that the loon used to nest on the lake. They decided that they needed to do something.

An article on the Loon Fund inspired them, and the national organization provided them with information and ideas to get the local group going. From a six-person start (more than the number of loons in the state), an organization was born. They began to watch the loons seriously. They saw the spring migrants, and then they saw them disappear two weeks after the beginning of the fishing season.

The group bought slide/tape and videocassette presentations, and they even held a loon conference. They got people to build loon nesting platforms, and they garnered statewide publicity. They held fund raisers and got a community to join them in their "walk day." From a town that has a population of 300 in a sixty-mile radius, a new consciousness was born.

As an offshoot to this program, the group got involved with a local teacher who worked with them in the development of a reading program. The program encourages the students to read many things, including nature-oriented materials. The students make a mural, and the fastest reader gets to add the loon and nest to the mural. In addition, the program gives out a T-shirt that has a mother loon with spectacles reading a book that is set in parted cattails. On the nest are a bright-eyed chick and a yawning sibling; behind is a colorful sunset over a lake. The caption is "Loons love reading."

Many positive ideas and actions come from such an effort. The state nongame division has been involved with the group now, and the community recognizes and cares about the loon. You can stop at Robin's Cafe and Drive-in and see pictures of the loon and talk to people who have learned from the Loon Lake Loon Association.

If you care and if you want to do more, join an organization that understands the loon and can give you direction. Add your talents to the group, be a Loon Ranger, learn and teach. Observe, take action, speak for the loons.

The following are the organizations and individuals that we recommend contacting in the various loon areas.

Alaska Department of Fish and Game
333 Raspberry Road
Anchorage, AK 99502

Dr. Charles Trost
Biology Department
Idaho State University
Pocatello, ID 83209

Common Loon Protection Project
Maine Audubon Society
Rt. 1, Box 118
Falmouth, ME 04105

Paul Lyons
Metropolitan District Commission
485 Ware Road
Belchertown, MA 01007

Michigan Department of Natural Resources
Box 30028
Lansing, MI 48909

Minnesota Loon Preservation Project
506 Torrey Building
314 Superior Street
Duluth, MN 55802

Minnesota Nongame Division
Minnesota Department of Natural Resources
500 Lafayette Road
St. Paul, MN 55155

Minnesota Zoo
12101 Johnny Cake Ridge Road
Apple Valley, MN 55124

Loon Lake Loon Association
P.O. Box 75
Loon Lake, WA 99148

Montana Loon Surveys
Don Skaar
816 N. Ewing
Helena, MT 59601

Loon Preservation Committee
Main Street
Humiston Building
Meredith, NH 03253

North American Loon Fund
RR 4, Box 240C
High Street
Meredith, NH 03253

New York Loon Conservation Project
Audubon Wildlife Committee
Delmar, NY 12054

Judith McIntyre
Oikos Foundation
Syracuse University at Utica
Utica, NY 13502

Vermont Institute of Natural Science
Woodstock, VT 05091

Northwoods Wildlife Center
Minocqua, WI 54548

Wisconsin Project Loon Watch
Sigurd Olson Environmental Institute
Northland College
Ashland, WI 54806

Ontario Lakes Loon Survey
Long Point Bird Observatory
P.O. Box 160
Port Rowan, Ont.
Canada N0E 1M0

(P. Roberts)

BIBLIOGRAPHY

Why do we include a big bibliography in our book? We do it for you—the reader, the next author to tackle the loon, the next researcher. We do it for those who want to dig deeper, for those who have specific questions that our book does not answer.

Each writer puts forth an accumulation of knowledge that comes from many sources. Our sources are in our acknowledgments, the list of organizations, and this bibliography.

The literature on the loon has progressed dramatically in the last decade. In previous decades, the loon was one of the many birds in the general references. There was Bent's summary of the loon, which was part of his exhaustive project that included "state of the art" knowledge of all our bird species. That 1919 publication was augmented by a booklet from the Minnesota Ornithologists' Union that was sold in tourist areas. But there was no exhaustive study until Tom Klein's *Loon Magic*, which caught the spirit of the loon's phenomenal rise in popularity and put current scientific knowledge in order.

Other smaller books followed, but for us, Joan Dunning's book was the one that captured the bird's life in the most pleasant account. It was very personal, but also very accurate.

We hope our book is a good companion to these. It incorporates ideas from all the references in the bibliography, but it certainly does not capture all the knowledge that they represent. Our goal was to add more understanding, new knowledge, and challenge and to interest you so that you would read more.

Alvo, Robert. "Marsh Nesting of Common Loons (Gavia immer)." *Canadian Field-Naturalist* 95 (1981): 357.

Alvo, Robert. "Lost Loons of the Northern Lakes." *Natural History* 95 (1986): 58–65.

Arbuckle, Jane, and Lee, Melissa. "1985 Maine Loon Count: Aerial and Ground Methodology and Results." North American Loon Fund.

Armstrong, Edward. *The Folklore of Birds*. Boston: Houghton Mifflin Co., 1959.

Barklow, William. "The Functions of Variations in the Vocalizations of the Common Loon." Ph.D. diss., Tufts University, 1979.

Barr, J. F. "Feeding Biology of the Common Loon in Oligotrophic Lakes of the Canadian Shield." Ph.D. diss., University of Guelph, 1973.

Bartlett, Jen, and Bartlett, Des. "Diary of a Loon Watcher." *National Wildlife*, Jan./Feb. 1981, 40–46.

Beebe, William. "Notes on the Early Life of Loon Chicks." *The Auk* 24 (1907): 34–41.

Bent, Arthur. *Life Histories of North American Diving Birds*. Reprint. New York: Dover Publications, 1919.

Bergman, R. D., and Derksen, D. V. "Observations on Arctic and Red-throated Loons at Storkersen Point, Alaska." *Arctic* 30 (1977): 41–51.

Brewster, William. "The Loon on Lake Umbagog." *Bird Lore* 266 (1924): 309–15.

Brown, Dee. *Teepee Tales of the American Indian*. New York: Holt, Reinhart and Winston, 1979.

Brush and Clark, editors. *Perspectives in Ornithology*. Cambridge: Cambridge University Press, 1983.

Burroughs, John. *Leaf and Tendril*. Vol. 8, John Burroughs Complete Nature Writings. New York: Wise and Co., 1908.

Campbell, T. R. "Loon Concentration on Mille Lacs Lake." *The Loon* 42 (1970): 36–37.

Choate, Ernest. *The Dictionary of American Bird Names.* Boston: Gambit, 1973.

Cleaver, Elizabeth. *The Loon's Necklace.* Toronto: Oxford University Press, 1977.

Cracraft, Joel. "Phylogenetic Relationships and Monophyly of Loons, Grebes, and Hesperornithiform Birds, with Comments on the Early History of Birds." *Systematic Zoology* 31 (1982): 35–56.

Davis, Rolph. "A Comparative Study of the Use of Habitat by Arctic Loons and Red-throated Loons." Ph.D. diss., University of Western Ontario, London, Ontario, 1972.

Dunning, Joan. *The Loon.* Dublin, New Hampshire: Yankee Books, 1985.

Eckert, Kim. "First Spring Record of Pacific Loon in Minnesota." *The Loon* 58 (1986): 128–29.

Eckstein, Ronald. "Fostering a Loon Chick." *Passenger Pigeon* 42 (1980): 131–32.

Eriksson, Mats. "Acidification of Lakes—Effects on Waterbirds in Sweden." *Ambio* 13 (1984): 260–62.

Ewert, D. N. "Spring Migration of Loons at Whitefish Point, Michigan." *The Jack Pine Warbler* 60 (1982): 134–43.

Farrand, John Jr. "The Loon in its Summer Dress." *Audubon*, July 1984, 44–47.

Fichtel, Chris. "Loons, the Call of the Wild." *Vermont Life*, Summer 1984, 32–35.

Fichtel, Christopher. "The Breeding Status of the Common Loon in Vermont." Vermont Institute of Natural Science, Woodstock, Vermont, 1983.

Fitzgerald, Gerald. "Pleistocene Loons of the Old Crow Basin, Yukon Territory, Canada." *Canadian Journal of Earth Sciences* 17 (1980): 1593–98.

Garber, Clark M. *Stories and Legends of the Bering Strait Eskimoes.* Boston: Christopher Publishing House, 1940.

Gier, H. T. "The Air Sacs of the Loon." *Auk* 69 (1952): 40–49.

Gilroy, Norman. "Field-Notes on the Nesting of Divers." *British Birds* 12 (1923): 318–21.

Graham, Frank Jr. "Mystery at Dog Island." *Audubon*, March 1984, 30–33.

Harrison, Peter. *Seabirds.* Boston: Houghton Mifflin Co., 1983.

Haseltine, S. D.; Fair, J. S.; Sutcliffe, S. A.; and Swineford, D. M. "Trends in Organochlorine and Mercury Residues in Common Loon (Gavia immer) Eggs from New Hampshire." *Transactions of the Northeast Section, The Wildlife Society* 40 (1983): 131–41.

Henderson, A. D. "The Common Loon in Alberta." *The Condor* 26 (1924): 143–45.

Henderson, Carrol. *Woodworking for Wildlife.* St. Paul: Minnesota Department of Natural Resources, 1984.

Hier, Perry, P.; and Sperry, M. "Tumor on Loon." Minnesota Department of Natural Resources, Nongame Division, 1983.

Johnson, R. A., and Johnson, H. S. "A Study of the Nesting of Family Life of the Red-throated Loon." *Wilson Bulletin* 47 (1935): 97–103.

King, B. "Winter Feeding Behaviour of Great Northern Diver." *British Birds* 69 (1976): 497–98.

Klein, Tom. *Loon Magic.* Ashland, WI: Paper Birch Press, Inc., 1985.

LaBastille, Ann. "The Endangered Loon." *Adirondack Life*, May/June 1977, 34–38.

Lewin, Roger. *Thread of Life.* Washington, D.C., and New York: Smithsonian Books, 1982.

Locke, L. N.; Kerr, S. M.; and Zoromski, P. "Lead Poisoning in Common Loon (Gavia immer)." *Avian Diseases* 26 (1982): 392–96.

Mathisen, John. "Use of Man-made Islands as Nesting Sites For the Common Loon." *Wilson Bulletin* 81 (1969): 331.

Mays, Verna. "Voice of the Wilderness." *National Wildlife*, Dec. 1975, 28–33.

McIntyre, Judith. "Wintering Behavior of Common Loons." *Auk* 95 (1978): 396–403.

McIntyre, Judith. "Nurseries: A Consideration of Habitat Requirements during the Early Chick-Rearing Period in Common Loons." *Journal of Field Ornithology* 54 (1983): 247–53.

McIntyre, Judith. "A Louder Voice in the Wilderness." *National Wildlife*, Aug.–Sept. 1986, 47–51.

McIntyre, Judith, and Mathiesen, J. E. "Artificial Islands as Nest Sites for Common Loons." *Journal of Wildlife Management* 41 (1977): 317–19.

Munro, J. A. "Observations of the Loon in the Caribou Parklands, British Columbia." *Auk* 62 (1945): 38–49.

Nero, Robert. "Further Records of Summer Flocking of Common Loons." *The Blue Jay*, June 1972, 85–86.

Olson and Marshall. *The Common Loon in Minnesota.* Occasional Papers, no. 5. Minneapolis: University of Minnesota Press, 1952.

Palmer, Ralph, ed. *Handbook of the North American Birds.* New Haven: Yale University Press, 1962.

Parker, Karl. "Observations of a Flying Common Loon Carrying a Fish." *Journal of Field Ornithology* 56 (1985): 412.

Peterson, Margaret. "Breeding Biology of Arctic and Red-throated Loons." Master's thesis, University of California, Davis, 1976.

Peterson, Margaret. "Nesting Ecology of the Arctic Loons." *Wilson Bulletin* 91 (1979): 608–17.

Pittman, James. "Observations of Loon Air Flight Speed." *Wilson Bulletin* 65 (1953): 213.

Predy, Ronald. "Another Summer Concentration of Common Loons." *The Blue Jay*, Dec. 1972, 221.

Ream, Caterine. "Human Disturbance, Pesticide Residues in Northern Minnesota." *Wilson Bulletin* 88 (1976): 427–32.

Reimchen, T. E., and Douglas, S. "Observations of Loons (Gavia immer and Gavia stellata) at a Bog Lake on the Queen Charlotte Islands, Canada." *Canadian Field-Naturalist* 94 (1980): 398–404.

Reimchen, T. E., and Douglas, S. "Feeding Schedule and Daily Food Consumption in Red-throated Loons (Gavia stellata) Over the Prefledging Period." *Auk* 101 (1984): 593–99.

Ridgely, R. "The Common Loon on Squam Lake." *New Hampshire Audubon Quarterly* 28: 30–52.

Roberts, Thomas. *The Birds of Minnesota*. Minneapolis: University of Minnesota Press, 1932.

Robertson, I., and Fraker, M. "Apparent Hybridization Between a Common Loon and an Arctic Loon." *Canadian Field-Naturalist* 88 (1974): 367.

Romer, Alfred. *The Vertebrate Story*. Chicago and London: University of Chicago Press, 1959.

Rummel, L., and Goetzinger, C. "The Communication of Intraspecific Aggression in the Common Loon." *Auk* 92 (1975): 333–46.

Simons, Malcolm Jr. "Beached Birds Survey Project on the Atlantic and Gulf Coasts." *American Birds* 39 (1985): 358–62.

Sjolander, S. and Agren, G. "Reproductive Behavior of the Common Loon." *Wilson Bulletin* 84 (1972): 296–308.

Southern, William. "Copulatory Behavior of the Common Loon." *Wilson Bulletin* 73 (1961): 280.

Sperry, Mark. "Common Loon Attack on Waterfowl." Minnesota Department of Natural Resources, 1985.

Storer, R. W. "The Fossil Loon Colymboides minutus." *The Condor* 58 (1956): 413–26.

Storer, R. W. "Evolution in Diving Birds." Proceedings of the 10th International Ornithological Congress, 1960.

Strong, Paul. "Habitat Selection by Common Loons." Ph.D. diss., University of Maine, 1985.

Strong, P. I. V., and Lutz, B. W. "Strong Affinity to an Old Nest and Hatching of an Abandoned Egg by Common Loons." *Passenger Pigeon* 48 (1986): 74–75.

Sutcliffe, Scott. "Changes in Status and Factors Affecting Common Loon Populations in New Hampshire." Fish and Wildlife Conference, 1978.

Sutton, G. M. and Parmalee, D. F. "On the Loons Of Baffin Island." *Auk* 73 (1956): 78–84.

Tate, J., and Tate, J. "Mating Behavior of the Common Loon." *Auk* 87 (1970): 125–30.

Terres, John. *The Audubon Society Encyclopedia of North American Birds*. New York: Alfred Knopf, 1980.

Trimm, H.W. "Wilderness Profile." *Conservationist* 39 (1985): 36–37.

Valley, Paul. "Common Loon Density, Productivity, and Nesting Requirements on the Whitefish Chain of Lakes in North Central Minnesota." Minnesota Department of Natural Resources, Nongame Division, 1985.

Vermeer, Kees. "Some Aspects of The Nesting Requirements of Common Loons in Alberta." *Wilson Bulletin* 85 (1973): 429–35.

Vermont Department of Forests, Parks, Recreation and Fish and Game. "Unknown Status of the Common Loon in Vermont."

Woolfenden, Glen. "Selections for a Delayed Simultaneous Wing Molt in Loons (Gaviidae)." *Wilson Bulletin* 79 (1967): 416–20.

Yonge, Keith. "The Breeding Cycle and Annual Production of the Common Loon (*Gavia immer*) in the Boreal Forest Region." Master's thesis, University of Manitoba, Winnepeg, Manitoba, 1981.

Zimmer, Gary. "The Status and Distribution of the Common Loon in Wisconsin." *Passenger Pigeon* 44 (1982): 60–66.

INDEX

ABOUT THE AUTHORS

Mike Link has an enthusiasm for adventures—adventures as diverse as paddling a wild river, sailing the open seas, observing a wild bird, keying out a new flower, or reading a good book. Each experience is a challenge, and each new assignment is an opportunity. Mike has two children, Matt and Julie, who have shared outdoor experiences with their father.

As director of Northwoods Audubon Center, Mike also is an instructor in outdoor education for Northland College and the University of Minnesota at Duluth. His published works include *Journeys To Door County, The Black Hills/Badlands, Outdoor Education,* and *Grazing,* and numerous magazine and newspaper articles.

Kate Crowley's skills as a naturalist and writer were developed during her nine years at the Minnesota Zoo, where she supervised the monorail interpretive program and wrote articles for zoo publications. Her knowledge of wildlife and wilderness grew with participation in volunteer bird censusing for the Minnesota River Valley Wildlife Refuge and exploration of wild lands in the U.S. and abroad. She has served for five years on the board of the Minnesota Naturalist Association.

Kate is the proud mother of Alyssa and Jonathon. Her interests include almost any outdoor activity, especially sailing and bird-watching and more recently, exploring her new home in Willow River, Minnesota, with Mike.

Mike and Kate were married aboard the ketch *Izmir* and sailed Lake Superior on their honeymoon. They are coauthors of a new series for Voyageur Press covering wildlife and wild lands. *Love of Loons* and *Boundary Waters Canoe Area Wilderness* are the first two books in this series.

ABOUT THE PHOTOGRAPHER

Peter Roberts's photographic talent was first recognized in Ames, Iowa, by his ninth-grade earth science teacher for his "Sunrise over Skunk River." He went on to study biology at Bemidji State University in Minnesota and received a bachelor's degree in economics from the University of Washington.

Peter's work has appeared in *Airone, Das Tier,* *Defenders, Living Bird, Natural History,* and *National Wildlife* magazines and in books published by Audubon Books, Cartwheel Press, Chanticleer Press, Northwoods Press, and Voyageur Press, among others. He operates a stock photography business in Seattle, where he lives with his wife, Kim, and daughter, Emily.

(P. Roberts)